Cambridge Elements

Elements in Gender and Politics
edited by
Tiffany D. Barnes
University of Texas at Austin
Diana Z. O'Brien
Washington University in St. Louis

GLASS CEILINGS, GLASS CLIFFS, AND QUICKSANDS

Gendered Party Leadership in Parliamentary Systems

Andrea S. Aldrich
Yale University

Zeynep Somer-Topcu
University of Texas at Austin

Shaftesbury Road, Cambridge CB2 8EA, United Kingdom

One Liberty Plaza, 20th Floor, New York, NY 10006, USA

477 Williamstown Road, Port Melbourne, VIC 3207, Australia

314–321, 3rd Floor, Plot 3, Splendor Forum, Jasola District Centre, New Delhi – 110025, India

103 Penang Road, #05–06/07, Visioncrest Commercial, Singapore 238467

Cambridge University Press is part of Cambridge University Press & Assessment, a department of the University of Cambridge.

We share the University's mission to contribute to society through the pursuit of education, learning and research at the highest international levels of excellence.

www.cambridge.org
Information on this title: www.cambridge.org/9781009539579

DOI: 10.1017/9781009429894

© Andrea S. Aldrich and Zeynep Somer-Topcu 2025

This publication is in copyright. Subject to statutory exception and to the provisions of relevant collective licensing agreements, no reproduction of any part may take place without the written permission of Cambridge University Press & Assessment.

When citing this work, please include a reference to the DOI 10.1017/9781009429894

First published 2025

A catalogue record for this publication is available from the British Library

ISBN 978-1-009-53957-9 Hardback
ISBN 978-1-009-42986-3 Paperback
ISSN 2753-8117 (online)
ISSN 2753-8109 (print)

Additional resources for this publication at www.cambridge.org/EGAP_SomerTopcu

Cambridge University Press & Assessment has no responsibility for the persistence or accuracy of URLs for external or third-party internet websites referred to in this publication and does not guarantee that any content on such websites is, or will remain, accurate or appropriate.

Glass Ceilings, Glass Cliffs, and Quicksands

Gendered Party Leadership in Parliamentary Systems

Elements in Gender and Politics

DOI: 10.1017/9781009429894
First published online: April 2025

Andrea S. Aldrich
Yale University

Zeynep Somer-Topcu
University of Texas at Austin

Author for correspondence: Zeynep Somer-Topcu, zsomer@utexas.edu

Abstract: Using novel leadership data from eleven developed parliamentary democracies between 1980 and 2020, this Element asks how gender conditions party leaders' candidacy, selection, and survival. It examines the life cycle of party leadership careers of 276 leaders with a focus on three categories of variables: performance indicators, (s)election details, and inclusiveness of political culture. It tests the existing theories of glass ceilings and glass cliffs on how certain conditions make it more likely that women run for and are selected as party leaders. The Element also offers an original quicksand theory on leaders' survival in office that, for women, leadership is akin to being caught in quicksand. Several factors agitate the quicksand and make them sink faster. The authors data shows support for the glass ceiling and quicksand theories. Yet, they find mixed support for the glass-cliff theory. The Element offers unique insights into women's experience with party leadership.

Keywords: Party leadership, women leaders, leader survival, leader candidates, leader elections

© Andrea S. Aldrich and Zeynep Somer-Topcu 2025

ISBNs: 9781009539579 (HB), 9781009429863 (PB), 9781009429894 (OC)
ISSNs: 2753-8117 (online), 2753-8109 (print)

Contents

1 Introduction   1

2 The Party Leaders Dataset   9

3 Candidacy and Selection of Women Party Leaders   25

4 Tenure of Women Party Leaders   51

5 Conclusion   74

   References   79

An online appendix for this publication can be accessed at www.cambridge.org/EGAP_SomerTopcu

1 Introduction

In parliamentary democracies, party leaders hold a crucial role that extends beyond the traditional responsibilities of managing a political party. They are central to shaping government policies, determining cabinet composition, and influencing the overall direction of national politics (O'Brien et al. 2015; O'Neill, Pruysers, and Stewart 2021). The increasing personalization of politics, a trend observed across many parliamentary systems, has elevated the significance of the party leaders (Poguntke and Webb 2005; Cross, Katz, and Pruysers 2018). As the focus shifts from parties to individual leaders, their public image often becomes key for electoral success (Banducci and Karp 2000). This shift, often referred to as the "presidentialization" of parliamentary systems (Mughan 2000), has made leaders the primary faces of their parties, with media coverage and election campaigns increasingly centered around them (Poguntke and Webb 2005).

The impact of party leaders extends beyond election campaigns, persisting throughout their tenure in government. They play a decisive role in forming and sustaining governments and often define the policies their party pursues while in power (O'Brien 2015). Leadership changes within a party can significantly alter voter perceptions (Somer-Topcu 2017), and these perceptions significantly affect partisanship and voting behavior (Garzia 2011; Garzia, Ferreira Da Silva, and De Angelis 2022).

Given these increasingly pivotal roles party leaders play in the parliamentary systems, a growing literature aims to answer questions like how these leaders are selected (LeDuc 2001; Kenig 2009; Lago and Astudillo 2023), how different selection processes affect leader evaluations and party performance (Cozza and Somer-Topcu 2021; Cozza, Di Landro, and Somer-Topcu 2023), and what affects leaders' tenure in office (Andrews and Jackman 2008; Somer-Topcu and Weitzel 2023). Yet, only a few studies explore how the personal characteristics of leaders themselves interact with this process and have mostly focused on how specific personality traits of leaders affect their evaluations by the voters (see, e.g., Bittner 2011), and not on the gender of party leaders (saving the fine exceptions we cite in this Element).

Perhaps this paucity of leader gender focus occurs because party leaders are usually drawn from a similar pool of elite, white, and male political leaders, leaving little diversity among them. The advancement of women into political leadership positions, while significant, remains fraught with challenges and gendered dynamics that perpetuate inequality. Despite an increase in women's representation in national parliaments and cabinet positions globally, women continue to face barriers to attaining and retaining top leadership roles. Our data from 11 advanced parliamentary democracies covering 40 years show that only 58 of the 276 leaders across 53 political parties (about 20% of all leaders) have been women, and even fewer women have risen to the positions of heads of state or prime ministers (Huidobro and Falcó-Gimeno 2023).

Gender diversity in party leadership is important, and understanding the factors that affect their candidacy, selection, and tenure, therefore, is critical for several reasons. The presence of women in party leadership positions plays a pivotal role in advancing gender equality within political systems, impacting both the representation and the perception of women in governance. Women in politics have been shown to improve public perceptions of women's leadership, challenging traditional gender biases and making citizens more accepting of women in positions of power, such as in cabinets or as prime ministers (O'Brien et al. 2015). Their influence extends beyond their own parties, often creating spillover effects that encourage other parties in their countries to select female leaders (Jalalzai and Krook 2010; O'Brien and Piscopo 2019). They can significantly enhance both descriptive and substantive representation by increasing the number of female candidates and elected officials and by prioritizing policies that address social justice issues (Kittilson 2011; Kroeber 2022; O'Brien et al. 2015). Studies have shown that when women hold leadership roles, they foster greater participation and influence among other female politicians, such as in parliamentary debates (Blumenau 2021).

Given these important roles of women leaders, there is an urgency to study the life cycle of women in party leadership positions. Only a comprehensive analysis would allow us to better understand the factors that encourage them to run, get elected, and survive longer in office. Our Element aims to help with this inquiry and pave the way forward for potential prescriptions to help women run, win, and keep party leadership positions.

We are, of course, not the first to study women's leadership. Astudillo and Paneque (2022), Dingler and Helms (2023), Morgenroth et al. (2020), O'Brien (2015), O'Neill and Stewart (2009), and Thomas (2018) unpack the selection of women party leaders, showing the importance of performance, selection processes, and party-level factors, such as ideology, in helping women to control the party leadership. A growing literature examines the consequences of women leaders for political party positions (Kroeber 2022), voter perceptions of political parties (O'Brien 2019), women attaining cabinet positions and portfolios (O'Brien et al. 2015), and voter evaluations of party leadership (Bridgewater and Nagel 2020; Chen et al. 2023; Dassonneville, Quinlan, and McAllister 2021). Women's tenure in party leadership has attracted less attention but important work by O'Brien (2015) and O'Neill, Pruysers, and Stewart (2021) shows that performance and harsher standards cut women's tenure short. It is to this important and growing literature that we seek to contribute by examining when women run as candidates, become party leaders, and how long they stay in office.

Through the study of the candidacy, selection, and tenure processes of women versus men politicians, we examine two important theories developed in the gender and politics literature: the *glass ceiling* and *glass cliff* theories. The glass ceiling argument points to barriers preventing women from reaching higher positions, and previous research provides reasons to believe that the selection of leaders is a gendered process in several different ways. Access to political leadership positions, like cabinet posts, follows different patterns for men and women (Aldrich and Perez 2021; Davis 1997; Escobar-Lemmon and Taylor-Robinson 2009; Krook and O'Brien 2012). Within the party, gender bias could prevent party elites from recruiting members of the opposite sex for high-level positions (Niven 1998; Devroe and Van Trappen 2022). Women in leadership roles frequently encounter biases in recruitment and selection processes, and those who do break through the glass ceiling are more likely to be assigned to less prestigious cabinet positions or to step down following electoral setbacks (Baumann, Bäck, and Davidsson 2019; O'Brien 2015). Seminal work on party leader gender by O'Brien (2015) and O'Neill and Stewart (2009) shows that women are more likely to become leaders of parties on the left, those that are less competitive in elections or minor parties, and those that are losing seat share.

The latter finding that women are more likely to become leaders in difficult times is the main premise of the glass cliff theory. Women are often appointed to leadership positions in politically challenging contexts, such as when their parties are unpopular or facing crises, a phenomenon known as the "glass cliff" (Ryan and Haslam 2005, 2007; O'Brien 2015). The main rationale behind this theory is that a weak party is seen as a risky investment, and career-oriented men do not want to take the risk and run. Women in this context (for whom stereotypes may make other party elites think that they are not career politicians) are seen as sacrificial lambs, encouraged to "take one for the team" (Stambough and O'Regan 2007). Women may also want to capitalize on this context by running in these less competitive elections for a high-risk position to further their career (Armstrong et al. 2023).[1] All this creates a window of opportunity for women to run and get elected for an otherwise undesirable position, which we analyze in detail in Section 3.

---

[1] As Armstrong et al. (2023) emphasize, glass cliff theory does not suggest women have no agency – the circumstances a low-performing party creates can allow women to capitalize on an empty field, even though it is a high-risk position.

Once elected, how does women's tenure differ from men's? The average tenure across the two genders in our dataset is similar. The average tenure for women and men has been 5.5 and 5.6 years, respectively. Despite the similarities in tenure length, we argue the leader position is like *quicksand* for women, sucking and sinking them more quickly than the cement men rule on. Existing literature suggests gendered patterns for how women in office/high-rank positions are treated differently than men. Expectations about when and where women leaders are most competent are often conditioned by gender stereotypes (Davidson-Schmich, Jalalzai, and Och 2023). Women are rewarded when their leadership conforms to these expectations but are punished when they do not (Holman, Merolla, and Zechmeister 2011). This makes it more difficult for women to use their leadership power in assertive ways to solidify their control of the party. In addition, O'Brien (2015) presents comparative evidence that unfavorable electoral outcomes have more devastating consequences for women leaders. Voters also have gendered preferences for leaders under different crisis conditions, preferring male leaders in times of national security threats and women in more peaceful times (Lawless 2004), and women are often excluded from powerful positions in defense, finance, and foreign policy (Barnes and O'Brien 2018), which prevents them from gaining experience that allows them more authority in these areas as leaders. This literature suggests that potentially different factors come into play as parties decide to replace men and women leaders in office.

Our original *quicksands theory* for women's tenure argues that while performance in office has been cited as the main reason for party leaders (Andrews and Jackman 2008) and especially for women's shortened tenure (O'Brien 2015), the factors that agitate the quicksand and make women sink go beyond just performance. Women leaders often find themselves navigating an unstable political environment, much like standing on quicksand, where their position can be easily threatened by their performance, the specifics of their election, and the prevailing attitudes toward women in leadership. The obstacles they face are varied, including gender biases, unrealistic expectations, and doubts about their legitimacy. The quicksand they stand on can be easily disturbed by any of these setbacks, leading to potentially shorter leadership tenures for women. We unpack all these factors in Section 4.

Despite this growing research on women as party leaders we discussed earlier, we still lack a comprehensive analysis of how the party and system-level features affect the candidacy, selection, and removal of women party leaders. Building on this important work and pushing it forward, our goals in the research we present here are to test the glass ceiling, glass cliff, and quicksand theories for women leaders to understand (1) when leadership contests include women candidates, (2) when they become party leaders, and (3) what affects women leaders' time in office compared to men. Not only do we expand the scope of research on women and party leaders with the addition of our unique, cross-national data, but we also contribute a more detailed analysis of the complete leadership life cycle of both men and women. In what follows, we briefly present the three categories of variables that we will be using in the following sections to explain when women run for party leadership, when they get elected as leaders, and how long they last in office: (1) performance indicators, (2) (s)election details, and (3) the gender inclusiveness of the political culture.

Performance Effects

We argue that there are both demand-side and supply-side reasons for why women are more likely to run for party leadership and get elected to the party leadership position during times of weak party performance. On the demand side, party losses, particularly major losses, motivate parties to undertake a significant brand change for the party to signal the efforts the party is engaging in to recover from the losses and rise up from its ashes. A woman leader is a significant change in the party's brand, given the continuous rarity of women party leaders at the top of political parties. In addition, a woman would signal the salience the party gives to recovery, given that crises require more collaboration or consensus-building within the party, which is the type of leadership that women are typically perceived as being especially skilled at (Davidson-Schmich, Jalalzai, and Och 2023). On the supply side, men are less likely to run for party leadership when the party is performing weakly in order to save their faces and to wait until the party recovers. Building on the glass cliff theory, women are more likely to be elected to leadership positions when the party is experiencing a crisis (O'Brien 2015; Ryan and Haslam 2005). This change in the competition dynamics creates opportunities for women to run for and become party leaders (Beckwith 2015), even though they are often treated as sacrificial lambs in those circumstances (Stambough and O'Regan 2007).

Once elected as leaders, women are also more likely to lose their leadership positions for weak performance. The stereotypes of women not being effective leaders and not fit for leadership positions more easily play against women when the party performs poorly (Holman, Merolla, and Zechmeister 2011; O'Brien 2015; Perdue 2016; Yates 2019). Any performance downturns, regardless of their size and impact, would be more likely perceived as the woman leader's failure, increasing their likelihood of replacement. Hence, we argue, similar to O'Brien (2015) but taking her findings of the detrimental effects of seat change further, that a broader definition of performance that includes seat changes, government loss, polling losses, and a combination of these need to be taken into account to examine women's tenure.

Selectorate and Leadership Election Effects

Moving beyond party performance, we also argue that structural party-level factors, especially leader election details, have important consequences for who runs and becomes the party leader and how long they survive. Cozza and Somer-Topcu (2021) show that inclusive leadership elections increase the number of candidates and competition. While more candidates mean that the likelihood of women running for leadership increases with inclusive elections, there is mixed evidence on how much risk women will accept in a competition. On the one hand, some competition environments can deter women from running if they are more averse to a campaign environment that cannot guarantee truthful competition (Kanthak and Woon 2015). On the other hand, the ability to compete as individuals may encourage other women to be more risk accepting (Folke and Rickne 2016; Magalhães and Pereira 2024). Therefore, we do not have clear expectations for how the inclusive selectorates and the level of competition (i.e., the number of candidates) affect women's candidacy. Yet, we expect inclusiveness to negatively affect the likelihood of women getting elected to the leadership position. Selectorates that include members may use gender stereotypes as information cues (Fox and Oxley 2003) and may be less likely to agree on priorities that promote women to leadership (Kenny and Verge 2013) compared to more exclusive selectorates (Rahat and Hazan 2010).

While we expect inclusive selectorates to be less likely to elect a woman, we expect those women who clear this hurdle and become party leaders following inclusive elections, who defeat a large number of competitors, and who achieve all this with a high margin of victory to be more likely to stay in office for a long time. Our argument builds on the literature that shows that the selection process and the details of leadership elections (Cozza, Di Landro, and Somer-Topcu 2023) can affect the legitimacy of a leader's power (Astudillo and Lago 2021). If the selectorate is small, and the win is less impressive (with a small number of challengers or a small margin of victory), the choice of leader may be viewed as an elite and/or indirect mandate. Women are more likely to be susceptible to these negative effects of selectorate size on their tenure, given they may start at a more disadvantageous point compared to men in terms of their legitimacy as leaders, and these effects may be exacerbated if the selected leader performs weakly.

Gender-Inclusiveness of Political Culture Effects

Building on Krook and O'Brien (2012) and O'Brien (2015), we argue that a gender-inclusive environment, both within the party and in the broader political environment, increases the likelihood of women running for and getting appointed to party leadership. When a party has already had a woman as its leader, it would indicate a more welcoming environment for women who are considering running for party leadership. Parties that already have a large share of women in their parliamentary delegation will have a larger pool of qualified women. More inclusive national parliaments represent more gender-equal societies and provide examples of women's leadership in politics. The presence of women in institutions like parties and legislatures also has a role model effect on potential political aspirants (Wolbrecht and Campbell 2007) and can encourage more women to seek leadership roles. Thus, we posit that parties with previous women leaders and with a large share of women members of parliaments (MPs), and national parliaments with large numbers of women MPs are more likely to include women in the selection process for party leadership, more open to electing women leaders, and less likely to punish women in office. We also argue that the performance, selection, and political culture effects likely work in an interactive manner for women's candidacy decisions, elections to leadership, and survival in office. In Sections 3 and 4, we test how these factors separately and jointly affect women's careers at the top of the parties in advanced parliamentary democracies.

A Quick Glance at What's Coming

Our novel Party Leaders Dataset (details in Section 2) allows us to test our expectations across eleven parliamentary democracies, covering four decades of party history in most of these cases. Our results, therefore, provide generalizable evidence that can help us confirm or challenge existing arguments regarding the gendered nature of politics, especially at the top positions of the political parties in parliamentary democracies.

Our findings are very interesting, and while they support some of the existing expectations raised in the literature, they sometimes also go against some established arguments about women's political careers. First, we find that performance downturns, which have been cited as the most critical factor in helping women to get to the top positions, only impact women's *candidacy* and in interesting ways. Parties experiencing performance-related leadership resignations are more likely to include women in the next leadership contest, but we find no evidence that this effect carries through to leadership selection, contrasting the glass cliff theory expectations. In addition, when we use the more objective performance indicators, like seat change or government loss, we find that if any coefficient is significant, it is positive, indicating that parties that perform well are more likely to have more women as candidates or leaders. Women's tenure, on the other hand, heavily depends on performance downturns, particularly on seat losses and major losses. Second, the selectorate type, whether it is by membership or delegates, compared to more exclusive, elite-based selectorates, has conflicting results for women's likelihood to run for party leadership elections and women's success in leadership elections. Inclusive selectorates encourage women's inclusion in leadership contests (we see higher shares of women candidates in these elections) but negatively affect their selection as leaders. Party electoral structure, therefore, has contrasting effects for candidacy and selection of women. As opposed to our expectations that membership elections should help women's tenure by increasing their legitimacy evaluations, we find that they only help women if the elected leaders perform well in office, suggesting again that performance is a big driver of tenure.

In terms of competition, our unique data allows us to investigate how the composition of candidate pools for leadership and their size impacts each stage of a woman's leadership career. We show that competition follows very gendered patterns: when women are selected as leaders, they generally face less competition and are selected most often with no competition at all. As the number of men in a contest increases, women are far less likely to be elected. Thus, the candidacy stage is a crucial step for women. If they are included in leadership contests, they most likely win. For tenure, on the other hand, we show that the smaller the pool, the better for women's tenure. Given that most of the women leaders in our data did not experience any competition, this finding suggests that either women leaders take on a less-desirable position or are very high-quality and dominant powers that are not easily challenged in office. The margin of victory, on the other hand, does not affect tenure.

What is consistently very important for the candidacy and selection of women leaders is the gender-inclusiveness of the political culture. The parliamentary culture, specifically the shares of women MPs in the party and the national parliament, substantively and significantly increases the chances of seeing more women candidates and leaders, respectively. Interestingly, though, gender-inclusivity does not affect or condition the other factors for women's tenure. It appears that while the inclusiveness of the political culture is essential for the candidacy and selection of women, once they do break that glass ceiling, the cultural factors no longer impact their careers directly or through other key variables.

Finally, one of our most important contributions, which we unpack further later in this Element, is showing how women's careers as political party leaders have three distinct stages with their own gendered patterns. Inclusion in the leadership contest as candidates is crucial, but different factors affect these stages in varying ways, making it hard to make one-for-all prescriptions for women leaders. Once elected, their tenures are defined mostly by office performance, while the inclusiveness of the political culture no longer affects women.

Our results have important implications for, and contributions to, the scholarship on women's access to power and their careers in politics, intra-party politics, and political leadership in general. In addition to a rich empirical analysis of novel data on women's experience in party leadership, we also offer a rich theoretical story about the internal functioning of political parties. By going inside the "black box" of the party with data on internal selection processes, we are able to contribute to the understanding of how political parties work and how they navigate power struggles, as well as make a significant advancement of our knowledge of when and to what extent these power relationships are gendered.

In what follows, we first present the details of our Party Leaders Dataset (Section 2) and present some descriptive details about party leadership candidates, elected leaders, and their tenure in office. In Section 3, we focus on women's candidacy for and election to party leadership before we turn to the analysis of women's tenure in Section 4. We conclude in Section 5 with a summary of our findings, the implications of our results, and a discussion of further suggested directions to examine women leaders' careers in parliamentary democracies.

2 The Party Leaders Dataset

Before theorizing and systematically testing our expectations on when women run for party leadership, are elected as party leaders, and how long they last in office once elected compared to men, it is important to understand how political parties in advanced parliamentary democracies elect and replace their leaders and to descriptively examine how gendered party leadership elections and removals are. To that end, we have coded a novel dataset, Party Leaders Dataset (PLD), which covers party leadership details from eleven advanced democracies across forty years. These countries are Australia, Canada, Denmark, Germany, Ireland, the Netherlands, New Zealand, Norway, Spain, Sweden, and the United Kingdom. The dataset includes all political parties with at least 5% vote share in at least two consecutive elections between 1980 and 2020 and excludes those parties that have shared/dual leadership and those that had only one leader in this time period.[2] The interim leaders, who were placeholders

---

[2] If a party only had one leader between 1980 and 2020, that leader will be censored in our survival analyses due to the lack of termination. For this reason and to be consistent across the different sections, we opted to exclude those parties with only one leader during the covered period from the analyses.

Table 1 Countries and parties in PLD

Country	Party	Country	Party
Australia	Democrats	Netherlands	Christian Democratic Appeal
	Greens (2005–2020)		Democrats 66
	Labor Party		Green Left (1989–2020)
	Liberal Party		Labour Party
	National Party		People's Party
Canada	Bloc Québécois (1990–2020)		Socialist Party (1989–2020)
	Conservative Party (2004–2020)	New Zealand	Labour Party
			National Party
	Liberal Party	Norway	Centre Party
	New Democratic Party		Christian Democratic Party
	Progressive Conservative Party (1980–2003)		Conservative Party
			Labour Party
Denmark	Conservative People's Party		Progress Party
	Liberal Alliance (2007–2020)		Socialist Left Party
	Liberal Party	Spain	Citizens (2006–2020)
	People's Party (1996–2020)		People's Party
	Progress Party (1980–1999)		Socialist Workers' Party
	Social Democratic Party	Sweden	Centre Party
	Social Liberal Party (1994–2020)		Christian Democrats
			Left Party
	Socialist People's/Green Left		Liberals
Germany	Christian Democratic Union		Moderate Party
	Free Democratic Party		Social Democratic Party
	Social Democratic Party		Sweden Democrats (1989–2020)
Ireland	Fianna Fáil	United Kingdom	Conservative Party
	Fine Gael		Labour Party
	Labour Party		Liberal Democratic Party (1988–2020)
	Progressive Democrats (1985–2020)		
	Sinn Féin		

Note: The data for each party (unless specified differently) starts with the leader who was in office as of 1980 and ends with the leader who was in office as of 2020.

until the permanent leader was elected, are also excluded given their temporary role in party leadership. Table 1 shows the countries and political parties in PLD. If a party entered the data after 1980 or exited before 2020, the time period is coded next to the party name.[3]

The decision to exclude political parties with dual leadership was not an easy one, given the likely effects of this decision to exclude some important

---

[3] A few small parties had to be excluded despite achieving 5% vote share due to our inability to find data on those parties' leadership details.

women leaders and parties from our dataset. For instance, the German Greens have always had two leaders, and out of seventeen leaders since their formation in 1993, ten were women and seven were men. However, because these dual leadership elections often happen in a staggered manner when one leader is already in office, our theoretical expectations need to be modified for these cases because party rules and norms can influence the gender of the next leader. Thus, we leave the analysis of the dual leadership parties' leaders' selection and survival to future research. Nevertheless, we acknowledge that some important parties on the left, such as several Green parties, are excluded from our dataset due to this criterion. However, we still have a good variation of left and right parties in our dataset even when we exclude the dual leadership parties (eighteen left parties, nineteen right parties, and sixteen parties from liberal, agrarian, or ethnic party families).

Who is considered the party leader varies from country to country and even across political parties in the same country. While the party leader has a parliamentary seat and is the de facto leader of the parliamentary faction in many countries, the extraparliamentary party organization is more powerful in some countries. In Norway, for instance, the leader of the extraparliamentary party organization is the de jure and de facto leader of the party (Strøm 1993). In Germany, the party leader is often the Chancellor candidate of the party, but there have been exceptions. Gerhard Schröder, for example, was the Chancellor candidate of the Social Democrats (SPD) in 1998, while the de jure leader of the party was Oskar Lafontaine. In addition, in some countries, there is variation at the party level as to who the de facto party leader is. As Pedersen and Knudsen (2005) state, while the parliamentary group leaders are primarily considered as the party leaders in the Social Liberal Party and the Conservative People's Party, "the leader of the party organization is the leader in the case of the Socialist People's Party, the Social Democratic Party, the Centre-Democrats, the Liberal Party, and the Danish People's Party," who are elected by the registered party members in the parties' annual conferences (167). Despite these variations across the countries and the parties, in each of our cases, there is a common, agreed-upon understanding of who is considered the de facto party leader of the party. We decided on whom we should code as the de facto party leader based on our extensive reading of each case and, when in doubt, in consultation with country experts (i.e. political scientists in our case countries). Party Leaders Dataset provides the appointment and resignation information of these party leaders.

The data for PLD come from various sources. First, we read on each country and party case and decided on the list of de facto party leaders. Undergraduate students at Vanderbilt University and the University of Texas, Austin coded the details of party leaders (their demographic information), party leadership elections, and resignations using web searches, news articles (through the Nexis Uni database or country-specific news archives), and academic writings. Finally, we hired native-speaker undergraduate students in respective countries to fill in the missing data.

The dataset is the only dataset on party leaders that provides information on (1) the candidates who ran for party leadership, their gender, and performance, (2) the selection details for the party leaders (the candidates, the selectorate, and the election details), and (3) the reasons for their terminations. Here, we summarize these details and use these variables in the empirical analyses in the following sections.

Party Leader Gender

In total, our dataset codes 277 leaders' information. Among these, 58 identified themselves as women, and 219 were men. Table 2 shows the number of women and men politicians who were appointed as leaders in each decade and country.

Overall, we see that women are more likely to become party leaders after 1990 compared to the 1980s. However, interestingly, while the percentage of newly elected women leaders jumped from about 10% to 36% between the 1980s and 1990s, there were fewer women leaders getting elected in the 2000s, and the percentage of new women party leaders of the 1990s was not surpassed in the 2010s. Regarding country performances, the Scandinavian countries stand out. The United Kingdom, Ireland, and Spain, on the other hand, are the most male-dominant countries. Despite the long tenure of Margaret Thatcher as the Conservative Party leader in the UK between 1975 and 1990, there were only two women party leaders in the history of the UK parties after 1980, and those were Theresa May of the Conservative Party (2016–2019), and Jo Swinson, who became the first woman leader of the Liberal Democrats in 2019.[4] In Ireland, the first-ever woman party leader was Mary Harney, who was the leader of the Progressive Democrats between 1993 and 2006. The only other woman leader was Joan Burton of the Labour Party, who was elected in 2014 but resigned following the bad electoral performance in the 2016 election.

---

[4] Party Leaders Dataset's coverage starts in 1980 and therefore does not code the 1975 appointment details of Margaret Thatcher. Its coverage also stops before the appointment of Liz Truss and excludes the Scottish National Party because its vote share at the national level never passed the 5% threshold.

Table 2 Leader genders by Country and decade (men/women)

Country	1980s	1990s	2000s	2010s/2020s	Total	(%)
Australia	7/1	8/3	10/2	8/2	33/8	(80.5/19.5)
Canada	2/1	6/2	6/0	7/1	21/4	(84/16)
Denmark	2/1	7/3	4/5	6/3	19/12	(61.3/38.7)
Germany	3/0	7/0	6/1	3/2	19/3	(86.4/13.6)
Ireland	8/0	4/1	7/0	4/1	23/2	(92/8)
Netherlands	6/0	7/2	8/2	7/2	28/6	(82.4/17.6)
New Zealand	4/0	1/2	4/0	5/1	14/3	(82.4/17.6)
Norway	6/1	3/4	2/4	4/0	15/9	(62.5/37.5)
Spain	2/0	2/0	2/0	4/1	10/1	(90.9/9.1)
Sweden	5/1	5/2	5/2	4/4	19/9	(67.9/32.1)
UK	3/0	5/0	6/0	4/1	18/1	(94.7/5.3)
Total	46/5	55/19	60/16	60/19	221/59	
(%)	(90.2/9.8)	(64.3/35.7)	(79/21)	(76/24)	(78.9/21.1)	

Note: Each cell shows the number of men and women leaders in each country by decade. The last row and the last column show the total number of men and women leaders by decade and by country, respectively, along with the percentages of each gender.

Neither of the two major parties in Ireland, Fianna Fáil nor Fine Gael, had any women as party leaders. Similarly, neither the Socialist Workers' Party (PSOE) nor the Popular Party (PP), the two largest mainstream parties in Spain, had women leaders in their history. The only Spanish woman party leader in our dataset is Ines Arrimadas, who was elected as the party leader of the Citizens Party in 2020. Overall, the following parties never had a woman as a party leader (until 2020, the end date for our data): Australian Liberals and Nationals, Canadian Liberals and Conservatives, Danish Liberal Alliance and the Liberals (V), German Liberal Democrats (FDP), Irish Fine Gael and Fianna Fáil, Dutch Labor Party (PvdA), the Party for Freedom and Democracy (VVD), and Christian Democrats (CDA), Spanish Socialist Workers' Party (PSOE) and Popular Party (PP), Sweden Democrats, and the UK Labour Party. In terms of the party family performance for women leadership, the left parties in our dataset (the green, socialist/left-libertarian, and social democratic parties) had 109 new leaders between the late 1970s and 2020, and 27 of them were women (24.8%), the liberal and center parties appointed 70 leaders, 15 of which were women (21.4%) while the right parties (conservatives, Christian democrats, and far-right) appointed 91 leaders, 16 of which were women (17.6%), which suggest some ideological bias, whereby left parties are more likely to appoint women as their party leaders, as cited in the literature (see, e.g., Caul 1999; Dingler and Helms 2023).

We also checked when our parties had their first woman leader. The timing of the first woman leader can be an indicator of the gender-inclusive culture of the party (see the later discussion). While at least one woman in all of our countries (except Germany, Ireland, New Zealand, and Spain) was appointed to leadership either in the 1970s or 1980s, Germany had its first woman leader (Angela Merkel) in the 2000s, Ireland in the 1990s (the Progressive Democrats), New Zealand in the 1990s (Labour Party), and Spain in 2020 when the Citizens Party appointed Ines Arrimadas.

Finally, we note that when a woman is appointed as a leader, that does not guarantee that more women will be appointed party leaders to replace the women leaders. Out of 47 women leaders for whom we know their replacements, only 14 were replaced by a woman, while 33 were replaced by men. These numbers suggest on their surface that women's leadership is seen as more out-of-the-ordinary rather than norm-changing, suggesting descriptive evidence in support of the glass cliff theory we examine in detail later in the Element.

Candidacy and Elections for Party Leadership

The Party Leaders Dataset codes the information on all the candidates for and the details of the leadership elections. Our extensive research resulted in information on 272 leadership elections' candidate information. A total of 558 candidates competed for these 272 leadership positions. Not only were women less likely to be elected to party leadership, but women were also less likely to run for party leadership elections in our dataset. Out of 558 candidates in PLD, only 120 (21.5%) were women. We discuss why women are not running and when they are running in Section 3.

Despite these low numbers of women among the candidates, the good news is that women, when they do run for party leadership, get elected to office. Of the 120 women candidates in PLD 49% were elected as party leaders. Yet despite this good performance on the part of the women candidates, the literature suggests that things may not be all rosy for women. Thirty-two out of the 59 women leaders (54%) were elected in elections with only one candidate running for office. Party crisis and uncertainty can reduce competition for leadership by deterring male candidates from seeking the post (Beckwith 2015; O'Brien 2015). Thus, women will likely end up as the only candidates for leadership.

When it comes to electoral procedures, more parties across parliamentary democracies are giving more power to their party members in electing leaders. While four out of 50 leaders (8%) were elected by party membership in the 1980s, that number increased to 28 leaders out of 79 (35%) in the 2010s (21 of these leaders were elected solely by membership vote while seven leaders were elected by a combination of membership, delegate, or parliamentary votes). The most common selectorate for leadership still is party delegates. These party officials are often local representatives of parties and vote in party conferences to elect the next party leader. 109 leaders in PLD (39%) were exclusively elected by delegate votes. The next most common method is the vote by the party's parliamentary faction. Ninety-seven leaders in PLD were elected by the party MPs.

Table 3 shows the number of women and men leaders elected by different selectorates across the countries in PLD. The table shows, for instance, that no delegate vote exists in Australia or New Zealand, while all leadership elections are through delegate votes in Germany, Norway, and Sweden (with the exception of Rudolph Scharping's membership election to German SPD's leadership in 1993, which was later approved by the delegates in the party congress). Among women leaders, 10 were elected exclusively by the party membership (17% of all women leaders), 15 were exclusively elected by the MPs (25% of all women leaders), and 28 were elected exclusively by the party delegates (48%). These numbers suggest that the literature is onto something: party membership appears to not elect women, and most women are appointed by party delegates or party elites (although we should consider that Scandinavia, with its numerous women leaders and dominance of delegate elections, may be the reason for these numbers). We unpack these selectorate effects on leader gender further in the next section.

The final component of the leadership selection in PLD concerns the election details for leadership. Party Leaders Dataset codes the number of candidates competing in the elections, the vote shares of the winning candidates, and the top two candidates' vote difference in the first round of the leadership election. Among the 272 leaders in PLD for which we have the leadership election details, 144 were elected unopposed, and 63 leadership elections had three or more candidates. The 2017 Conservative Party leadership in Canada had the most crowded slate: 14 candidates ran in the election for which all registered party members were eligible to vote using a ranked ballot. In the end, Andrew Scheer defeated Maxime Bernier by 1.9% and won the leadership election with the support of 50.95% of the membership votes. As we described earlier, 32 out of the 59 women leaders (54%) were elected in elections with only one candidate running for office, which suggests that women leaders emerge out of less competitive elections. Does this mean that women are scapegoats in

Table 3 Selectorates and leader gender by Country

Country	Members Men/Women	Delegates Men/Women	Parliamentary Faction Men/Women	Party Leadership Men/Women
Australia	3(2)/6	0/0	32(31)/2	0/0
Canada	12(10)/0	9(7)/4	0/0	2/0
Denmark	1/2	10/3	8/6	1/0
Germany	1(0)/0	19(18)/3	0/0	0/0
Ireland	5(3)/1	4(2)/0	16(14)/1	0/0
The Netherlands	13/2(1)	2/0	13/4(3)	0/1
New Zealand	2(0)/0	0/0	14(12)/3	0/0
Norway	0/0	16/9	0/0	0/0
Spain	3/1	7/0	0/0	0/0
Sweden	0/0	19/9	0/0	0/0
United Kingdom	13(8)/2(1)	2(0)/0	11(4)/1(0)	0/0
Total	53(40)/14(10)	88(81)/28	94(82)/17(15)	3/1
%	79(80)/21(20)	76(74)/24(26)	85(84)/15(16)	75/25

Notes: The numbers show the number of men and women leaders who were elected by party membership (column 1), delegates (column 2), parliamentary faction/MPs (column 3), and party executive/leadership (column 4). The numbers in parentheses show the number of leaders who were *exclusively* selected by the respective selectorate, that is, multiple selectorates are not involved in the selection of the leader. The final row shows the percentages of each selectorate method used in the data for women versus. men leaders. For instance, the first column percentages show that 79% of all leaders who were elected via membership vote, and 80% of all leaders who were *exclusively* elected by membership vote were men, as opposed to 21% of the membership vote elected leaders who were women (and 20% of *exclusively* membership vote elected leaders).

difficult times when others are unwilling to take on the leadership position, consistent with the glass cliff theory? We will empirically test this theory in the next section.

In terms of vote shares of the top candidates, 108 leaders in our data (out of 253 for which we have data on election outcomes) were elected with unanimous support in the first round or by acclamation without any opposition. Three leaders in PLD had a very competitive first (or only) round of election with less than 1% vote margin compared to their competitors. Frank Clusky of the Irish Labour Party received 50% support against Michael O'Leary's 50% support in the first round of the leadership election (and won later in the second round with 56% of the MP votes compared to 44% support for O'Leary). Andrew Little of the New Zealand Labour Party (in 2014) and José Luis Rodríguez Zapatero of Spanish PSOE (in 2000) won their respective leadership positions in four-candidate races with less than a 1% vote difference to their closest competitor.

Table 4 Leadership election competition by gender

		Number of Candidates	Margin of Victory (or the vote share of the only candidate)
Women Leaders	Minimum	1	0.033
	Maximum	7	1
	Mean	1.78	0.719
	St. Dev	1.27	0.378
Men Leaders	Minimum	1	0
	Maximum	14	1
	Mean	2.12	0.64
	St. Dev	1.78	0.399

Notes: The table shows the minimum value, the maximum value, the mean, and the standard deviation of the number of candidates and the margin of victory (top-two candidates' vote difference) for women and men leaders. If there was only one candidate, the margin of victory is coded as the percentage of votes the winning candidate received.

Table 4 presents the number of candidates and the top two candidates' vote difference (in the first or the only round of the elections) for women and men in the dataset, which we call the *margin of victory*. If there was only one candidate, the margin of victory shows the vote share of the only candidate. The numbers show that women competed in less crowded slates (with an average of 1.7 candidates), while men leaders had slightly more competitors (with an average of 2.1 candidates). The most crowded competition that a woman won was the Canadian New Democratic Party's leadership election of 1989, when Audrey McLaughlin competed with six male candidates. When the first preferences were counted, McLaughlin had 27% of the votes against the 24% of the votes of David Barrett. In the last round, McLaughlin won with 55% of the delegate votes. The second column in Table 4 shows that, on average, women candidates received more votes compared to their competitors in the first (or the only) round of the election. On average, women received 72% more votes compared to their closest competitor (or 72% as the only candidate) in the first (or the only) round of leadership election, while men received 64% more votes. Twenty-seven of 52 women leaders (52%) for whom we have the leadership election results were elected unanimously or by acclamation, while only

40% of the men leaders were elected unanimously or by acclamation. These numbers suggest that when women run for leadership, they receive higher support and face less competition. While this may suggest good news for women, this evidence is also consistent with the glass cliff theory we cited earlier, which suggests that women often run for office in difficult times when no man wants to compete for a failing party's leadership.

Terminations of Party Leaders

In addition to the appointment details, PLD also provides the details on the length of tenure for each leader and the reasons for termination. In Section 4, where we analyze the factors that affect women and men leaders' duration in office, we use the data for 223 leaders and exclude those leaders who were in office as of 2020, the end of our data coverage, and those who died in office for the survival analysis. For these 223 leaders, the average duration in office was 5.6 years, with a standard deviation of 4.7 years. The longest-serving leader in the data is Gerry Adams of the Irish Sinn Fein, who was the party leader between November 1983 and February 2018. The leader who served in office for the shortest time was Kevin Rudd of the Australian Labor Party, who, despite an almost four-year term in the late 2000s, lasted only for 72 days in office for his second term after he took over the party leadership from Julia Gillard in 2013 and resigned after the 2013 election due to the party's weak performance in the elections.

Regarding gender differences, the leader tenures in our data appear to be similar across leader genders. While the average tenure of men in PLD is 5.6 years (5.5 years if we drop Gerry Adams) and ranges from 72 (Kevin Rudd) days to 34 years (Gerry Adams), women leaders in PLD had on average 5.5 years in office, with a range of 167 days for Els Borst-Eilers of D66 to 18.7 years for Angela Merkel of CDU (the average duration for women drops to 5.2 years if we exclude Angela Merkel).

Our dataset also codes each leader's reasons for resignation/termination. We used 13 categories to code the reason for resignation. These are: (1) death in office, (2) national/federal election loss, (3) other election loss (in local elections, EU elections, referenda, etc.), (4) declines in opinion poll standings, (5) losing in leadership elections following a challenge, (6) parliamentary no-confidence motion, (7) scandal, (8) health reasons, (9) other personal reasons, such as retirement, family, and others, (10) moving to a different office/taking a cabinet position, (11) intraparty pressure, (12) merger with or split from a different party, and (13) other reasons that do not fit into any of these categories, such as the collapse of the coalition government or making way for new blood in the party.

There is often more than one reason why a leader resigns, and in those cases, multiple of these categories are coded for the leader. For instance, Diedrich Samsom of the Dutch PvdA was challenged and lost in the leadership election for his reelection following a decline in the opinion polls. Both decline in opinion poll standing (3) and loss in leadership election (5) were coded for his resignation.

For the analyses in the selection/candidacy section, we also coded these resignation reasons into one variable: performance-related resignations (if the resignation was due to national/federal election loss, other election loss, declines in opinion poll standings, and scandals), as opposed to any other reason. In our dataset, 68.2% of all women leaders resigned due to performance-related resignations, while 73.4% of men resigned due to performance-related events.

One other note on the resignation reasons is that these more qualitative codings of resignation reasons come from newspaper articles and secondary literature and do not necessarily correlate highly with actual party performance. For instance, the New Zealand National Party's leader Don Brash resigned in 2006 mainly due to a forthcoming book about his leadership but also due to the previous election outcome. We coded the resignation reasons as scandal and national election loss. However, in reality, the National Party increased its vote share by 18% and its number of seats by 21 in the 2005 elections. Yet, the outcome of the election was still seen as a failure, as the National Party was unable to unseat the Labour Party as the largest party in the parliament. We raise this point here because later we use these qualitative resignation reasons along with more objective performance indicators: seat changes, government status changes, and polling status changes. We explain how we code these variables in the next section.

Gender-Inclusive Political Culture

Following a growing literature, we argue that women are more likely to run for, win leadership positions, and keep those positions if the political culture of the country and their party is women-friendly and if the women have already shattered the political glass ceiling. In the following empirical sections, therefore, we add four variables to our models that we argue are good indicators of women-friendly culture and also test their conditioning effects on our other variables: (1) the parliamentary share of women MPs (at the level of country-parliament), (2) the party share of women MPs (at the level of each party), (3) whether a party already had a woman as their leader, and (4) the existence of party-level gender quotas.[5]

---

[5] While we call these variables indicators of an inclusive political culture, we note that they are more about the descriptive representation of women. Political culture is a controversial topic

Table 5 Parliamentary share of women MPs

Country	1980s	1990s	2000s	2010s
Australia	4.65	12.10	25.37	26.55
Canada	8.50	17.37	21.09	24.77
Denmark	26.33	33.88	37.72	38.35
Germany	11.09	24.86	31.90	34.68
Ireland	7.07	11.37	13.07	16.64
Netherlands	17.61	28.24	37.54	38.49
New Zealand	11.14	22.99	30.98	32.64
Norway	30.05	37.42	36.96	40.05
Spain	7.32	17.82	33.07	37.86
Sweden	30.94	38.59	45.37	44.82
UK	4.19	11.51	18.79	26.35

Notes: The table presents the average percentage of women MPs in each country by decade.

The shares of women politicians in the parliament (*Parliamentary Share of Women MPs*) and within each party (*Party Share of Women MPs*) are critical indicators of the women-friendly political culture within the whole parliament and each party, respectively. The existence of high numbers of women MPs in the parliament and parties breaks down the traditional norms for women, allowing them to seek leadership positions. The higher shares of women MPs also increase the supply of women by allowing for a larger pool of likely women candidates for leadership (Dingler and Helms 2023; Barnes and O'Brien 2018; Verge and Astudillo 2019). We extend this argument beyond the parliamentary share of women MPs and use data on women MPs in each party in our dataset to measure party-level inclusive culture, which we argue should be more significant for intra-party politics and leadership elections.

The data for the parliamentary share of women come from Paxton, Green and Hughes (2008) through 2003, and Barnes and O'Brien (2018) and the Women in Parliaments Dataset[6] for the remaining years. The data codes the share of all MPs who were women in each parliamentary period. Table 5 shows

in political science, and in no way can we claim that we perfectly measure political culture. However, for simplicity reasons, we call all these factors women-inclusive political culture indicators.

[6] http://archive.ipu.org/wmn-e/classif-arc.htm

the percentage of women MPs in each of our countries by decade. The numbers suggest that in each country there are more women MPs in the 2000s and 2010s, compared to the earlier decades. Denmark, Norway, and Sweden also stand out as having the highest shares of women MPs throughout the decades, although Germany, the Netherlands, and Spain appear to have caught up with the Scandinavian countries' numbers in the 2010s.

The party-level share of women MPs dataset mainly comes from Weeks et al. (2023); however, these data did not include Australia, Canada, and New Zealand. We collected the data for New Zealand from the parliamentary archives[7] and coded it for gender using the World Gender Dictionary.[8] Canadian data are available in their archives.[9] Data from Australia are taken from Alexander (2021). Figure 1 shows the box-whisker plots for the shares of women MPs by parties across the decades in each country. The larger the difference between the parties in terms of the shares of women MPs they have,

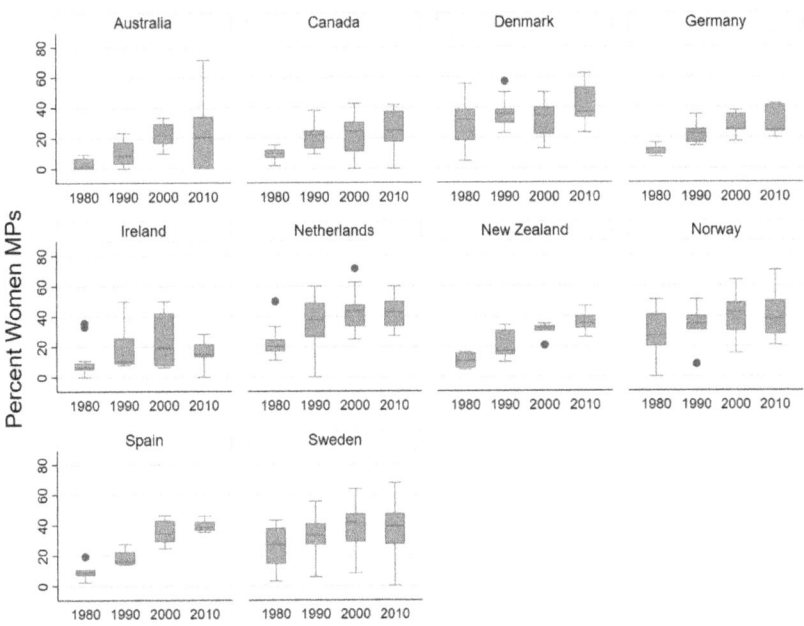

Figure 1 % of women MPs by party.

Notes: Each graph shows the box-whisker plots of the share of women MPs by party across the four decades of the data in each country.

---

[7] www.parliament.nz/en/visit-and-learn/mps-and-parliaments-1854-onwards/ accessed on May 14, 2024
[8] https://doi.org/10.7910/DVN/MSEGSJ
[9] https://lop.parl.ca/sites/ParlInfo/default/en_CA/People/parliamentarians accessed on May 14, 2024

the longer the box-whisker plots. The horizontal lines in each box show the median value in the data, whereas the upper border of each box shows the 75th percentile, and the lower border of each box shows the 25th percentile value in the data. The extreme outliers are represented with dots.

Overall, we see, similar to Table 5, that the share of women has increased in every country compared to the 1980s and 1990s. However, there is quite a lot of variation across parties and countries. For instance, despite the high variation in the share of women MPs across parties in the Netherlands in the 1990s, the variation declined and the median share of women was around 45% in the Dutch parties in the 2000s and 2010s. In Australia, on the other hand, the median share of women MPs was very low in the 1980s. The median share of women MPs by party increased to 20% in the 2010s with a much larger variation across the parties.

One way to increase the share of women MPs in the party is by introducing gender quotas. Gender quotas generally require a specific subset of an electoral list to be populated by women candidates, which are shown to be linked to the greater descriptive representation of women (see, e.g., Aldrich and Daniel 2025; Franceschet, Krook, and Piscopo 2012; Krook 2010; Schwindt-Bayer 2009). We use party-level gender quotas as another proxy for the gender-inclusive political culture.

The data for party-level gender quotas come from the Gender Quota Database[10] and Aldrich and Daniel (2024). In our dataset, 13 political parties have had gender quotas, and these are listed in Table 6 along with the first year the quota appears in our leadership data. We added a dummy variable for those political parties that had a gender-quota for the years they have had the gender quota.

The history of having a woman leader is another party-level women-inclusiveness measure that we use as a women-friendly culture indicator. Electing the first woman leader shatters the political glass ceiling in a party and indicates a visible break from the male-dominant past party politics (Matthews and Whiting 2022). We expect that when a party already had a woman as its leader in the past, it is possible that the increased scrutiny that the first woman leader receives in office likely softens for the successor women leaders. We coded *Ever Woman* as a dummy variable. It was coded 1 in the candidacy and selection data for those periods when the new leader election happened following the first woman leader. In the survival data, the variable was coded 1 for every month and year after the first woman leader left the office.

---

[10] www.idea.int/data-tools/data/gender-quotas-database

Table 6 Party gender quotas

Country	Party	First Year in Data
Australia	Labor	2010
Canada	New Democratic Party	1988
Germany	CDU	2017
Germany	SPD	1998
Netherlands	PvdA Labor Party	1998
New Zealand	Labour Party	1993
Norway	Christian People's Party	1993
Norway	Labor	2001
Norway	Left Socialists	1985
Norway	SP Centre Party	1989
Spain	PSOE Socialist Workers' Party	2011
Sweden	M (Moderates)	2014
Sweden	SAP (Social Democrats)	1994

Notes: The table shows the thirteen parties that had a party-level gender quota and the start year of the quota rule.

Modeling

Our interest in the whole life cycle of women party leaders, from the point when they decide to run as leader candidates to the leadership election and eventually to their termination, requires us to generate separate datasets and apply different modeling decisions in the following sections. While we explain the details of each dataset and the modeling choices in more detail in each section, a short overview is in order.

In the selection section, we code four different dependent variables to capture women's participation in the leadership selection process. To explore the gender dynamics of leadership candidacy, we use a binary measure of whether the leadership selection contest includes at least one woman candidate and also a continuous measure of the share of women candidates in the contest. To examine when women get elected as leaders, we use the gender of the winning leader as our dependent variable. We model this with a sample that uses all of our data (DV: leader-all) and also with a sample restricted to only contests that include women candidates (DV: leader-inclusive), excluding 177 contests that had no women candidates. We use logistic regression models for our binary variables and OLS regression for the share of women candidates dependent variable.

In the survival section, the data are coded in months. The unit of analysis is month-year for each party in each country. The leader resignations and appointments are coded as dummy variables for their respective months. The key variable to set the data as a survival dataset is the duration variable, which is coded 0 for the month of the appointment and increases one by one for each month until the resignation month. We use Cox proportional hazard models to test our hypotheses.

We include several control variables in our models. In addition to the performance, selectorate, leadership election details, and gender-inclusive political culture variables, our models also include a *Left* party control given left-wing parties and left ideologies are more supportive of gender-inclusive practices. We also control for Leader-Centric systems, by adding a dummy variable for Australia, Canada, Germany, Ireland, and New Zealand where party leaders have been more forefront and hence different strategic calculations may be in play. We also add a dummy variable for the 2000s and 2010s to control for the more recent improvements of women representation in party leadership.

We note that, due to the small number of women leaders compared to men in PLD, we expect to see large standard errors for women leaders. To make better inferences about our results, we use 90% confidence intervals to present our results in the remaining sections.

Conclusion

Our novel dataset covers 40 years of leadership changes across 11 parliamentary democracies and is a unique resource for those who are interested in understanding who runs for party leadership, how leaders get elected, and how and why their tenures come to an end. As we presented in this section, PLD shows when women (compared to men) run for office, how they perform in leadership elections, how long they last as party leaders once elected, and why they resign.

The descriptive evidence of this section points to seven preliminary conclusions, which we further unpack in the following sections. First, we see that party leadership is still a male-dominant position, especially outside the Scandinavian countries, and while there have been more women elected to the party leadership position after 1990, the numbers have not further improved over time. Second, we see that left parties are more likely to appoint women to their leadership positions. Third, women are not less likely to lose the leadership elections if they run, but they do not make it to the candidate level in greater numbers. Women are still underrepresented among the candidates. Fourth, when it comes to who is selecting the leader, party delegates are more likely to elect a woman candidate for party leadership compared to party membership and parliamentary factions. Fifth, women candidates face less competition and are elected to leadership positions with higher vote shares. Sixth, women and men have similar tenures in office. Finally, we see overall more women MPs across our country cases as time passes. However, there is still quite a large variation across countries and across parties in various countries in how gender-inclusive the political culture is.

We now move to the more systematic analyses of the candidacy, appointment, and termination details. The next section unpacks the candidacy and selection processes for women and men leaders, while Section 4 closely examines the tenure and termination of party leaders.

3 Candidacy and Selection of Women Party Leaders

Margaret Thatcher, the United Kingdom's Conservative Party's first woman leader and the country's first woman Prime Minister, became the party leader in 1975. Her leadership followed a tumultuous era for the Conservative Party. Having held the majority following the 1970 election but leading the party to two electoral defeats in 1974, losing their majority, and being unable to form a government, the party needed new leadership. However, many men were unwilling to challenge Edward Heath, and Thatcher, a candidate as equally qualified as any of the elite party men stepped up (Beckwith 2015). Thatcher won the leadership, eventually becoming the Prime Minister in 1979. She would go on to serve the longest term in modern history, nearly 15 years, until 1990 when facing opposition from within the party, she succumbed to party pressure and resigned.[11]

Decades later in July 2016, Theresa May became the second woman leader of The Tories. Her tenure as the party leader (and the PM) began after the unexpected "leave" vote in a national referendum on whether the UK should leave the European Union. Prime Minister David Cameron had called the referendum expecting to appease the anti-EU faction within the party and silence them with a pro-EU victory. This strategic calculation proved disastrous after the public voted to leave the EU. Citing a clear message from the public and facing turmoil within his party, Cameron stepped down immediately. Out of several names mentioned for the leadership position, Theresa May emerged as the top candidate because the leadership election "was not about the nature of the ship (the British state) nor its direction – because the ship is unstable and the course

---

[11] *The Guardian* December 12, 2018, Accessed June 29, 2019.

is uncharted waters – so it has had to be about who was better equipped to be captain" and "the captain must be a character who is steady, determined and reassuring."[12] Thus, like Thatcher, May came to power in a time of crisis.

Here are two different women presented with an opportunity to pursue leadership under similar circumstances. Both preceded men who had faced public defeats. Thatcher took over a country with a troubled economy, while May took over the leadership of a very divided party and an arguably divided public. Would these two women run for leadership and would they get elected to the top position if the circumstances were different? In this section, we examine whether there are factors that make it more likely for women to run for party leadership and the circumstances under which they win these positions.

We argue that gender plays an important role in both stages of leadership selection: (1) candidacy for and (2) selection to party leadership. Women and men who make it to party leadership generally have distinguished careers in politics already, which may lead us to expect that gender plays a smaller role in intra-party leadership elections. In terms of ambition, research has generally found women to be less willing to run for electoral office than men (Lawless 2004) because, for example, traditional gender norms socialize women and men into different beliefs about their place in society (Conover and Gray 1983). Survey research has also shown that women are less likely to feel qualified for office than men (Fox and Lawless 2011) and women are more averse to conflict that comes along with the electoral process (Kanthak and Woon 2015; Schneider et al. 2016). In low-informaton national elections, gender is a heuristic that may encourage stereotypes to play a role in candidate evaluations (Sanbonmatsu 2002). However, these don't automatically transfer to leadership elections. Most party leadership contests should contain more information about candidates, since winners will need to garner the support of party elites and/or membership. Thus, gender stereotypes should be less relevant. Party members considering leadership usually already have high political knowledge, so we expect there to be less doubt among women about their qualifications. Most importantly, any woman considering leadership has already broken through the candidate barrier. Thus, we wouldn't expect gender differences in ambition at this point (Davidson-Schmich 2015; O'Brien et al. 2015) and it may even be the case that women are less risk averse than men in terms of pursuing opportunities (Magalhães and Pereira 2024). Yet, despite these expectations, we still see very few women running for leadership and only a minority number of party leaders being women. The question is why is the glass ceiling still there?

---

[12] *Newsweek* July 12, 2016, Accessed November 21, 2023.

This section investigates if and/or when women are more likely to run for and to win leadership posts. We do so by exploring whether the relationships between performance, selection, and gender-inclusiveness of the political culture on the one hand and leadership and leadership candidacy on the other hand are gendered. We find that party performance, the selectorate for the party leader, leadership election details, and gender-inclusiveness of political culture are linked to women's fate in party leadership in nuanced ways. Our results show that performance downturns increase the likelihood of women running for leadership, consistent with the glass cliff theory, but the results do not generalize to all performance downturns or women's actual selection to leadership. Selectorate type has competing effects on inclusion and selection. An inclusive/membership-based selection process is associated with a higher likelihood that women will run as candidates but it is negatively associated with their success in becoming leaders. In mixed-gender contests, as more men compete for leadership, the likelihood that women win decreases. One place where we do find consistent support across both processes is that gender-inclusive political cultures increase the likelihood of women candidacy and leadership. Our most important contribution, and one we are uniquely positioned to make, given the novelty of our data, is that the conditions that impact the candidacy of women are not the same conditions that impact their success in winning. Thus, we encourage future work to continue to explore the intra-party dynamics of selection and not overlook the process for the outcome.

When Do Women Run for and Win Party Leadership?
Electoral Loss and Challenges to Party Reputation

Party performance crises can come in many different forms, but losing in national, regional, or local elections or government status are the most common factors for leaders to be replaced. Andrews and Jackman (2008) find that the party leaders' survival chances dramatically decrease after a loss of seat shares in an election in Westminster systems. Ennser-Jedenastik and Schumacher (2015) find that losing control of the government is also a surefire way to be removed as leader. Each of these losses can bring about a crisis in the party, and elites can look for new strategies to refocus the party and improve its image, precisely the kind of change that can be achieved with a new leader. Losing vote share or governing office is not the only time that parties confront crises in the public eye. Parties and leaders can become unpopular at any time in the election cycle, and problems with public opinion can also bring about change. In a cross-national study of over 12,000 public opinion polls across 45 countries,

Walther and Hellström (2019) find that public support is significantly related to the probability of leadership replacement.

Not only have crises been shown to be an impetus for party leadership change, but there is evidence that these types of crises are associated with better opportunities for women. Beckwith (2015) provides convincing evidence that this was indeed the case with the selection of Thatcher in the late 1970s, when Thatcher entered as a candidate for leadership with only one other man challenging Heath.

Overall, the literature suggests two reasons why women are more likely to run as candidates and win leadership elections when performance is down. O'Brien (2015), for instance, shows that parties are more likely to appoint a woman for the first time when they are losing seat share, as a sacrificial lamb in difficult situations, and also because of the need for more substantial change. Building on this work and the glass cliff theory (O'Brien 2015; Ryan and Haslam 2005 Ryan and Haslam 2007), we argue these unfavorable conditions within organizations and parties suggest a higher risk of potential leadership failure. This high-risk context leads men, who otherwise are plenty among the party elite circles and have higher chances of winning leadership positions, to stay out of the leadership race. In addition to this unwillingness of men to run at crisis times, women may be even more encouraged to seek leadership if party elites are signaling a time for a change or a renewal. In a study of women's paths to executive power, Norris (2010) found that women were viewed as symbols of change or renewal across six different case studies. These instances resulted in women becoming successful executive leaders after men had failed, providing evidence that women can capitalize on party downturns. Ryan, Haslam, and Kulich (2010), in a study of the UK election in 2005, also found that women were more likely to run in less winnable seats, signaling that at least on some level, women are willing to put themselves forward in these scenarios more often than men. So, while pursuing leadership during uncertain times is always risky, and even though men and women may view this risk in similar ways, women may be more willing to capitalize on the opportunity given the paucity of "good" opportunities for high-level leadership at other times (Ryan et al. 2016).

The second part of our argument is about party brand renewal. It might also be the case that the times of crises are the times when parties seek new strategies and are more likely to deviate from their status quo (O'Brien 2015). When the status quo is male leaders at the helm of the party, a change in party leader gender would signal that the party is willing to undertake significant change. Because women are associated with renewal (Norris 2010), women running for party leadership and winning the position would signal that the party is doing its best to overcome its performance downturn.

If we argue that entering the contest is a strategic move that women make when the opportunities are right, then it should follow that women will have a higher probability of winning. In fact, in our data, in contests that contain at least one woman, women win in 60% of our cases. This suggests that women are able to accurately gauge their chances of winning leadership over half of the time. Thus, if it is the right time for women to run, we also expect it is the right time for women to win. It may also be the case that this is known by men who opt not to compete with women under these circumstances or whose candidacy is not publicly embraced by the party because they prefer women. This leads us to our first hypothesis:

> *H1: Women are more (less) likely to run for and become party leaders when the party performance is poor (strong).*

But should we expect these performance effects to work the same across different performance indicators or contexts? First, we argue that major losses (as opposed to smaller/less detrimental losses) are more likely to result in a high number of women candidates and leaders because the risk of leadership is higher. Thus, a major loss, such as significant seat share loss and/or a change in government status may be necessary for a gender change in party leadership.

Second, we also argue that the political culture of a party and country conditions how performance affects women's candidacy and leadership. O'Brien (2015) shows the gendered effects of performance on parties' decisions to elect the *first-ever* woman as their leader. This implies that the performance effects are larger in less women-friendly environments where a woman leader is seen as a drastic change in the party's image. In addition, in order to run and get elected, politicians first need to advance their careers in the party and the parliament (Dingler and Helms 2023). Having a large pool of women MPs improves the chances of women running and winning party leadership positions. Therefore, we expect the performance downturns to increase the likelihood of seeing women candidates and leaders in less women-friendly systems when there was no previous woman in party, the share of women MPs is low, or when the share of women in the national parliament is low.

> *H1a: The effects of performance on women's candidacy and leadership are likely stronger when the party suffers major losses.*

> *H1b: The effects of performance on women's candidacy and leadership are likely stronger in less gender-inclusive political cultures.*

Selection Mechanisms and Institutional Deterrents

In addition to performance-related causes of leadership change, institutional barriers exist with respect to the nomination of women leadership candidates and their appointments as leaders. Organization of recruitment and selection and the environment of the decision-making process have an impact on women's access to leadership (Funk, Hinojosa, and Piscopo 2019; Verge and Astudillo 2018). We argue that who selects the leader and how many candidates compete in the election affect the likelihood of women running for leadership and their election to the party's top office.

In most party leadership selection processes, potential candidates need to show initial support from some party officials, whether that be the members of the parliamentary faction of the party or delegates in party local branches. So, when a woman sees an opportunity to step forward, she needs others to agree that this is the right time and establish a broad enough coalition to garner enough support. The performance-related conditions can determine the right time, but party elites may also consider other factors when choosing to support women for office that can be extended to leadership positions. In addition to implicit or explicit bias for certain types of candidates (see Niven 1998), men may also have better access to networks within the party and among potential party selectors that can advantage them in leadership contests (Bjarnegård 2013; Verge and Astudillo 2018). Thus, we might expect men party leaders to favor men candidates, all else equal, which can impact an individual's decision to seek leadership or gain the necessary support. So even though we know that women's progressive ambition in politics is similar to men's, they may face more structural barriers, like the selection environment, in realizing their ambition.

We build on Kenig (2009) to differentiate between different selectorates–who selects the leader–and their potential impact on women, ranging from most inclusive with membership vote to most-exclusive (in our dataset, the most exclusive system is when the top party leadership decides on the next leader). Allowing the party's registered members to vote in party leadership elections through the one-member-one-vote system is increasingly more common for party leadership across parliamentary systems. Most leaders in our dataset, however, are elected by either party delegates (about 40% in our data) or parties' parliamentary faction (also about 40%). Delegate elections are still inclusive as they include local branch representatives to vote in party leadership elections, although not as inclusive as the one-member-one-vote systems. Parliamentary faction and party leadership votes, on the other hand, are more exclusive, elite-based elections for party leadership.

How does the inclusiveness of the electorate affect women's *candidacy* for party leadership? On the demand side, there is evidence that inclusive leadership elections have more candidates (Cozza and Somer-Topcu 2021). If there are more candidates, there are simply more opportunities for women to be among them. Each candidate, man or woman, can have the opportunity to develop their own coalition of support among the masses instead of relying on party elites. Yet, because who becomes a candidate is often a function of individual political connections. If the party executive or the parliamentary party has control over the selection, women may be more likely to come forward if they are already members of the parliament or the party executive. These have access to elite networks and understand when conditions within the party are ripe for change (which suggests a conditional relationship between selectorate and candidacy, depending on the presence of women in politics, a point to which we return later). In addition, membership elections may also foster a type of competition that is less appealing to women. We know that women are more averse to competitive selection, even when they are equally qualified (Kanthak and Woon 2015). When inclusive elections are more crowded and competitive, often with the blood-on-the-floor effects of these primary elections, women may not find this appealing or worthy of their participation. At the same time, as Astudillo and Paneque (2022) state, membership elections, by their virtue of being inclusive, may allow selectors to focus more on competence and narrow the gap between women and men candidates (Folke and Rickne 2016). This gives women agency to campaign for themselves and their particular strengths. For all these reasons, we argue that the size of the pool may encourage or discourage women from running for leadership (i.e., we do not have clear expectations regarding the size of the pool/number of candidates).

On the supply side, the goal of diversifying the leadership competition field may indicate that elite-dominant parties may be more likely to encourage women to run and support the women candidates in these leadership elections (Matthews and Whiting 2022). In addition, an exclusive group of elites may be better at crafting 'package deals for better descriptive representation' (Bashevkin 2009; Verge and Astudillo 2019, 723). Aldrich (2020), in a study of candidate lists for European Elections, finds that candidate selection conducted by the executive of the party was more likely to yield women candidates than selection by mass membership, suggesting that party elites support women more than party members.

These are a lot of "ifs" we cannot test in this project due to data limitations. We argue that the number of candidates running for leadership and inclusive elections may increase or decrease the number of women candidates due to all these pull and push factors (H2 below). Nevertheless, one implication of the arguments we raised earlier is that we should see exclusive selectorates as especially conducive to more women candidates in leadership elections in women-friendly contexts with a high descriptive representation of women (H2b below).

Regarding the *selection* of women to leadership, we build on Astudillo and Paneque (2022) to argue that an inclusive selectorate makes it less likely for women to win. The intra-party elections for party leadership provide the same party cue (as opposed to the parliamentary elections), which forces people/members to use other heuristics for their decisions. This may activate stereotypes for some members and cause others to rely on heuristics that disadvantage women (Astudillo and Paneque 2022; Fox and Oxley 2003). A smaller group of party elites, on the other hand, can work together to push for the outcome they most favor (Rahat and Hazan 2010), which, according to the glass cliff theory, will sometimes be women. The party elites would also have more information on the leadership candidates and their qualities, potentially reducing the impact of stereotypes on women candidates. Finally, name recognition works better for established party elites, who are mostly men, disadvantaging women, and the same is true for media reporting of these elections, which have been shown to advantage men over women politicians (Hazan 2010; Astudillo and Paneque 2022).

We also expect the party performance and political culture to moderate the selectorate effects on women leaders. If the glass cliff theory is correct and performance downturns increase women leaders, then the negative effects of inclusive selections on women's leadership should dissipate, and the positive effects of exclusive selectorates should exacerbate in difficult situations for the party. In addition, regarding the gender-inclusiveness of the political culture, if women have made strides into politics and the stereotypes against women politicians have weakened, the negative effects of membership elections on women's likelihood to win should weaken in more gender-inclusive political contexts.

Our second set of hypotheses on the relationship between the structure of the selectorate and women's leadership candidacy and selection are as follows:

> *H2: Women may be more or less likely to run for party leadership with inclusive selectorates but are less (more) likely to get elected when the selectorate is inclusive (exclusive).*

> *H2a: The positive (negative) effects of an exclusive (inclusive) selectorate on women's elections to leadership are likely stronger (weaker), if there is a performance downturn.*

H2b: The positive (negative) effects of an exclusive (inclusive) selectorate on women's elections to leadership are likely stronger (weaker), if the politics is more gender-inclusive.

Cultural and Institutional Conditions for Women's Leadership

In addition to considering the decision-making environment and organization of the selection procedures, we have stated how important it is to consider the gender-inclusiveness of political culture as it conditions the performance, selectorate, and election effects. But beyond its conditioning effects, we argue that the more gender-inclusive the politics is, the better the chances for women to run and win leadership positions. To that end, the history of women within a party is an important determinant of the networks in which women can rise up through the ranks. Not only does the number of women in leadership positions determine the size of the pool for women leaders (Escobar-Lemmon and Taylor-Robinson 2016), it also determines the resources available to women when seeking higher office with respect to their networks (Bjarnegård 2013; Verge and Astudillo 2018). Thus, one possible encouragement for both women's candidacy and the selection of women leaders is the number of women in current leadership positions or among the party elite. While data on the composition of party executives can be difficult to collect, we can identify parties that have previously had women leaders. Thus we consider the impact of women predecessors and account for whether a party has ever had a woman leader at the time of a leadership change. Similarly, we also expect women to be more likely to both challenge party leadership and become party leaders when there are more women in the party's parliamentary delegation or the national parliament. Party quotas should also encourage women's political leadership by opening space for women in the party elite and its elected positions. When women's representation is high in the party or parliament, the pool of women politicians in the national political space is larger and differences between men and women in politics are less pronounced. Thus, our last hypothesis is as follows:

H3: Gender-inclusive political culture is more likely to be associated with more women running for and getting elected to party leadership.

Research Design

Overall, as explained in Section 2, men leaders are more abundant in the data. They make up roughly 79% (219 out of 277 leaders), and women are about 21% (58 in our dataset) for contests that result in a leadership change. In our sample of leadership contests, men replacing men are the most common at about 67%

of the sample. In the remaining sample, it is most common for women to replace men (~16%), then men to replace women (~12%), and finally for women to replace other women (~5%). This demonstrates that not only are women leaders less prevalent, but they are also less likely to appear in succession.

One unique feature of our data, as we stated in Section 2, is that in addition to identifying women who succeeded in becoming leaders, we also have data on the candidates who ran for the position of party leader. While we only have 58 women leaders when leadership change occurs, we have 96 leadership contests that include at least one woman candidate (*women inclusive contests*). Thus, our analysis uses both women's success in obtaining leadership positions and women's presence in leadership elections, which we use to generate four dependent variables– two for candidacy analyses and two for leadership analyses.[13]

To explore the gender dynamics of leadership candidacy, we use (1) a dependent variable (coded 0/1) for whether the leadership selection contest includes at least one woman candidate (*women inclusive contest*) and (2) the share of women candidates in the contest (*share of women*). To capture women's election to leadership, we use the gender of the new leader as our dependent variable but code it in two separate ways: (1) we code the leader gender (0/1) using all leaders' information in our data (*leaders-all*) (N = 277), and (2) we code the leader-gender (0/1) using only those leadership elections in which there were women among the candidates (*leaders-inclusive*) (N = 96). We use logistic regression models with robust standard errors for our binary variables (*women inclusive contest, leaders-all,* and *leaders-inclusive*) and OLS regression with robust standard errors for the *share of women*. However, we note that we should be cautious with our conclusions for the *share of women* dependent variable for the candidacy models as nearly 80% of our selections contests have either a zero share of women (65.4%) or only women (13.8%). This is in line with our expectations and with the glass cliff theory that the conditions that encourage women's inclusion in leadership contests may also discourage men. For most of our data, there are either women or men. Thus, we believe the models with the *women inclusive contest* DV are more informative.

We use several variables to test our performance hypotheses. First, we use the *performance resignation* variable that is coded 1 for those cases when the previous leader resigned for performance reasons based on the more qualitative data relying on their resignation statement or media coverage of the

---

[13] Descriptive statistics and an analysis of their relationship to our dependent variables can be found in Section A of the online Appendix.

resignation. Resignations are coded as performance resignations if election loss (parliamentary, local, EU, or referendum losses), declines in opinion poll ratings, or scandals are mentioned as the reason for resignation. We focus only on those cases whose resignations were coded as solely performance-related based on our qualitative codings. The more objective measures of performance indicators we use are: seat changes, government loss, and polling changes. We operationalize electoral performance as the change in parties' electoral performance between the two most recent elections (*Seat Change*) immediately before the leadership election. We use the change in seat shares rather than the change in vote shares, given that several of our country cases use plurality electoral systems, in which seat shares are more meaningful. The seat shares data come from the ParlGov dataset. Second, we include a dummy variable at the party level coded 1 if the previous leader lost the governing party status (*Government Loss*), also from the ParlGov data. To assess the effects of polling status, we calculated the change in party standing compared to the election performance in the last parliamentary election (*Poll Change*) immediately before the leader selection. The polling data come from Jennings and Wlezien (2016) and are updated to 2020. Given that we have a large number of missing values in the polling data, we run our models separately with and without the polling performance variable.

To test the selectorate hypotheses we use two independent variables: (1) *Members* is coded as a dummy variable for the leadership elections when the party's registered members through the one-member-one-vote system elect the new leader, and (2) *Members & Delegates* is coded as a dummy variable for cases where either the registered members or party delegates (or both) can vote for party leadership. We consider these as inclusive elections, the latter being a broader definition of inclusiveness, and compare these selectorates to more exclusive selectorates of parliamentary delegation or party executive electing the new leader. For the size of the candidate pool, we use the number of male candidates (rather than the total number of candidates) (*Male Candidates*). We choose not to use the total number of candidates because this measure includes women candidates. Since two of our dependent variables (*Women Inclusive Contest* and *Share of Women*) measure women's presence in the leadership contest, including them in the total number of candidates measure would be akin to predicting the effect of competition that includes the same women.

Finally, we use four gender-inclusive political culture indicators to test our H3 for the direct effects of political culture, which we described in detail in the previous section: (1) Ever Woman, (2) Share of Women MPs in Party, (3) Share of Women MPs in Parliament, (4) Party Gender Quota. However, when we include the political culture variables as control variables in the models, we only use the first and second measures because we argue that they are theoretically the most salient variables for women's candidacy and elections to party leadership. In addition, the party and parliamentary share variables and the quota and party share variables have high correlations.[14]

Our models also include several control variables. First, we include a dummy variable for the left parties of greens, left-libertarians, socialists, and social democratic parties. Following Bashevkin (2009) and Caul (1999), we expect women to be more likely to become candidates and leaders in left parties. We also control for the previous leader's gender as we expect that women are more likely to replace men and men are more likely to replace women, especially when a big change is seen as essential. Third, we add a dummy variable for the leader-centric countries, Australia, Canada, Germany, Ireland, New Zealand, and the United Kingdom, where the party leaders are more forefront compared to many proportional representation (PR) systems in Europe (*Leader-Centric*) and the decision on who will run for the leader position and who will get elected have more important consequences. Fourth, we add a dummy variable, coded 1 for the 2000s and 2010s, given that women are increasingly more likely to run in recent decades (*2000s and 2010s*). Fifth, we control for the time that has passed since the last election. We expect parties to be more careful about and less willing to take risks about who they will appoint as the time passes since the last election and as the time to the next scheduled election approaches. Finally, as we stated above, we control for the two cultural variables: the share of women MPs in the party and ever-woman.

Results for Candidacy and Leadership

Performance Effects

We first report the results of our performance-based measures for candidacy and leadership. We model this in three ways. First, we examine the relationship between resignations that were reported to be only due to performance reasons (*Only Performance Resignation*) and women's likelihood to run for and get elected to party leadership positions. To recap, these are coded based on the coders' readings of the resignation announcements and their coverage in the media. We expect women should be more likely to find an opportunity or to be encouraged to *run* and to *win* the party leadership when the previous leader resigned due to a performance reason. If women are capitalizing on performance downturns as opportunities for leadership and men are shying away from leading troublesome parties, we should see more *women inclusive*

---

[14] The descriptive analyses of all these variables are presented the online Appendix.

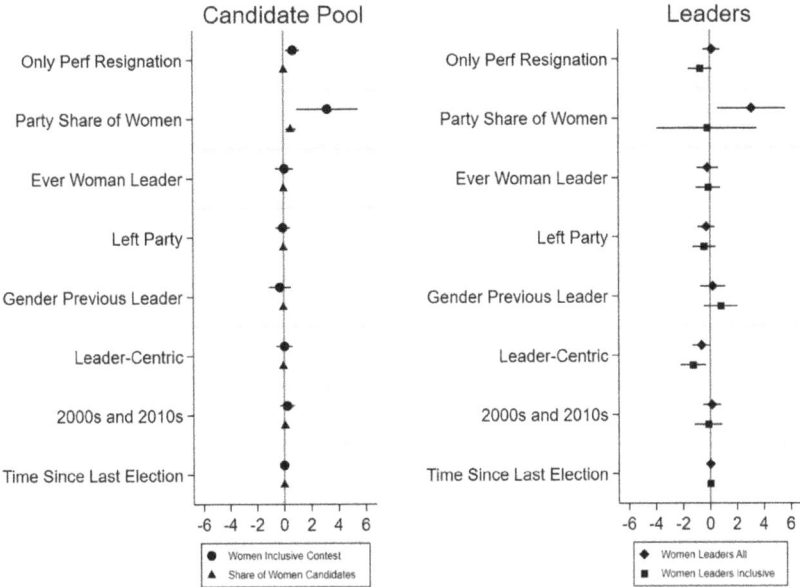

Figure 2 Performance Resignations
Note: The coefficients and the standard errors (with 90% confidence intervals) come from the fully specified models.

contests and a greater *share of women candidates*. Figure 2 reports the results of the models of the candidate pool on the left and for elected leaders on the right. The former includes models of *women inclusive contests* (circle) and the *share of women candidates* (triangle), while the latter includes women leaders in all contests (*leaders-all*) (diamond), and women leaders in the inclusive contest sample only (*leaders-inclusive*) (square).

The results show that performance-only resignations are a significant and positive predictor of women entering the leadership contest (*women inclusive contest*). Following the performance-only resignations, the predicted probability of a women-inclusive contest increases by about 15% (from about 29.5% following non-performance resignations to about 44.4% following performance resignations). This provides preliminary evidence in support of the glass cliff and political opportunity theory supporting the idea that women enter leadership contests when the party claims it has removed its leader for poor party performance and that leadership contests exclusive to men are less likely. However, there is no evidence of a relationship with the share of women candidates. In the second model (triangle), the only significant predictor of the *share of women candidates* is the percentage of women MPs in the party. The share of women in a leadership contest increases by about 5% for every 10% increase in the percentage of women MPs in the party.[15] This variable is also a significant predictor of the selection of women leaders in all contests (diamond). Here, the probability of selecting a woman leader increases by an average of 6% for each 10% increase in the share of women MPs in the party. For example, the probability of a woman winning leadership is about 9% when there are no women MPs and about 45% when women are at the max share (about 71%).

In the leadership model on the right, performance resignations do not seem to matter. These variables are not significant in the full sample (diamond) or the restricted/inclusive sample (square). In these models, the best-performing predictor is *leader centric*. Contests in leader-centric systems are significantly associated with a decreased probability of selecting a female leader in the restricted sample. Interestingly, in Section 4, we show that these rare women leaders in leader-centric systems have significantly longer tenures.

To sum up these findings, we have some evidence to support H1 (women candidates and leaders are more likely in poorly performing parties) in terms of women's candidacy and only for one of the two DVs, but not in terms of their likelihood to win. While this provides somewhat mixed evidence for our hypotheses, it tells us that the process for encouraging women candidates may be distinct from selecting them.

The next set of models test the performance effects by focusing on more objective measures of performance: *Seat change*, *Lost Government*, and *Polling Change*. Because we lose a significant number of cases with the polling data, we run these models separately with and without the polling data. Figure 3 reports the results of our models for the substantive variables and the significant control variable of share of women MPs in the party (the full models with controls are available in Tables A.7 and A.8). In Figure 3 we see that seat change is a significant and positive predictor of women leaders (diamonds and squares) in both leader models and for the share of women candidates DV (triangles).[16] However, this result goes against our expectations and, hence, against the glass cliff theory. For example, the share of women candidates actually increases from about 18% at a 10% seat loss, to about 27% when there is a 10% seat gain (see Figure A.1). The predicted probability of a woman leader (DV: leader-inclusive) is about 47% when a party experiences a 10% loss in seat share and increases to about 71% with a 10% seat gain (these probabilities are similar in our model that includes polling). These patterns remain the

---

[15] Full results, including reporting of the control variables, are available in Table A.6 of the online Appendix.

[16] It does lose significance when we add polling data for the share of women candidates and the full sample of leaders.

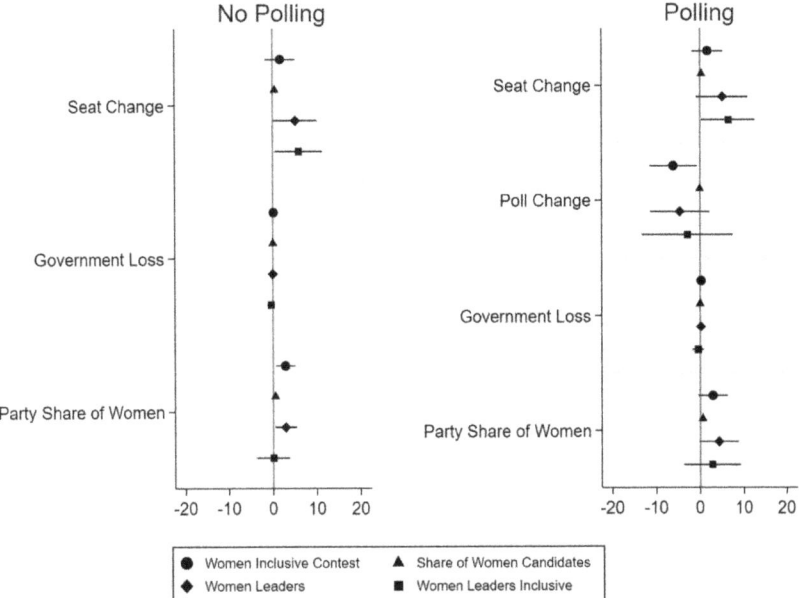

Figure 3 Objective Performance indicators' effects on women's candidacy and selection.

Note: The coefficients and the standard errors (with 90% confidence intervals) come from the fully specified models, including the control variables. The left-side graph shows the effects of seat change and government loss and the right-side graph adds the effect of polling change along with the effects of the other variables.

same in our full sample of leader-all DV (diamond), although the predicted probabilities are much smaller, about 14% and 30%, respectively.

These results mean that, at least in our data, women are chosen at times when parties are doing well and not just when they are performing poorly as the glass cliff theory expects. Seat changes are positively related to women's candidacy and election. At the same time, neither government loss nor polling change variables have statistically significant effects on women's candidacy or leadership. We also report the results of the share of women MPs in the party variable because it is the only control variable in these models that is significant and positively related to women's presence in leadership contests.

While these results do not fully conform to our first hypothesis, that women are more likely to run and become leaders when performance is poor (H1), it may be because there are differences in these relationships depending on whether a party is experiencing a minor or a major loss, as our H1a states. The glass cliff theory suggests that women are more likely to be seen as sacrificial lambs or may take on a high-risk opportunity after a major loss when no man is willing to step up. However, our data tells us that only slightly more than half of the leadership changes occur after any seat losses (about 68%), and just about 14% occur after a seat loss and loss of the government. Hence major losses are not that common in our selection data, yet we model the effect of a major loss and the combination of a major loss and loss of government. These models are reported in the online Appendix in Tables A.9, A.10, A.11, and A.12. In the models, our variable for major loss is not significant. However, some interesting insights come out of the combination of major loss and government loss models. Most notably, we are unable to include this variable in any of our leader models because we do not have a single observation of a women leader selected (and only 19 men) when a party lost both the government and at least 10% of their seat share. While there are 20 leadership changes following a major seat loss, only five of these new leaders are women. Thus we do not find evidence to support H1a using our major loss framework. However, our seat and government loss-based major loss variable is negatively associated with the share of women candidates. The predicted percentage of women candidates falls from about 22% to 13% when parties experience both a major loss and loss of the government. Overall, our evidence of the glass cliff hypothesis remains mixed and mostly negative. Performance resignations encourage women's inclusion in leadership selection, but all other measures do not seem to matter or, in fact, decrease the likelihood of women running for and winning elections.

Selectorate Effects

Our second hypothesis concerns the selectorate effects. To recap, we expect inclusive selectorates (compared to more exclusive/elite selectorates like the parliamentary faction and party elites) to select more men than women for party leadership positions, although we don't have clear expectations for how these inclusive elections affect women's candidacy.

To test this hypothesis, we run the models separately for delegate and membership elections and membership only elections, compared to all other types of selectorates. Figure 4 reports these results for our four models and shows that both measures of inclusive selection are associated with a positive likelihood of a women's inclusion (top left). Member and delegate elections are associated with about a 14% increase in the probability of an inclusive contest, and member-only elections are associated with nearly a 28% increase compared to elite selection. On the other hand, the selectorate does not appear to impact the share of women candidates (top right). We stated in the theory section that we did not have clear expectations for how the selectorate should affect women's candidacy (H2), and the evidence, at least from the top-left graph, suggests that an inclusive selectorate increases the likelihood of women's candidacy.

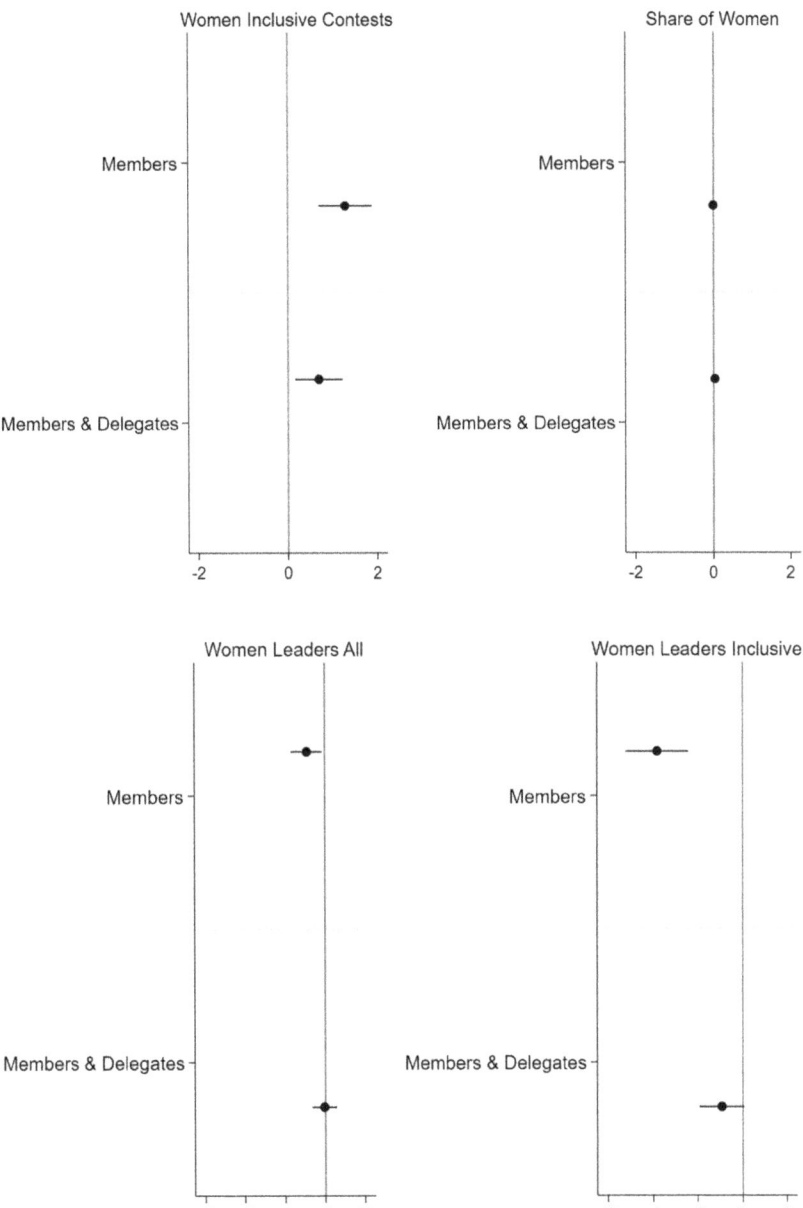

Figure 4 Selectorate deatils' effects on women's candidacy and selection.

Note: The coefficients and the standard errors (with 90% confidence intervals) come from the fully specified models, including our control variables.

The selectorate type has the opposite effect on the elected leader's gender, however, supporting our H2. In our full sample and our inclusive sample, member selection is negatively associated with the selection of women leaders. The predicted probability of a women leader decreases by ~11% for the full sample and nearly 64% in the inclusive sample when members choose the leader. The members & delegates selectorate coding, on the other hand, produces no significant (on the left) or weaker (on the right) negative effects on women leaders. This is not surprising given that (as we reported in Section 2) we see delegate elections, which are very common in Scandinavian countries, elect quite a number of our women leaders. The full models are available in Tables A.13 and A.14 in the online Appendix. This difference between the candidacy and leadership results is striking because it provides us evidence that the selection conditions (particularly membership elections) that foster women's inclusion (candidacy) make it less likely that they will be chosen. The negative effect on leaders in the women-inclusive sample (where women's predicted probably of winning drops from 80% to 16.7% when membership elections are used relative to executive selection) is more than double the size of the positive effect on women's inclusion in the contest (28% increase in the likelihood of inclusion following membership selection vs. executive selection).

Election Effects

Here, we test the effects of electoral conditions, particularly the number of candidates, on women's inclusion and selection; however, we did not set clear expectations for these effects. While we know some types of competitive elections can discoursage women candidates (Kanthak and Woon 2015), the openness of the candidate pool to more candidates may encourage more women to come forward. We use the number of male candidates (*Male Candidates*), as we explained in the previous section.

Figure 5 shows that the number of male candidates has a negative and significant relationship with women's leadership. While it is not significantly associated with inclusive contests (circle), as the number of male candidates grows, the share of women decreases (triangle). The predicted share of women in the contest is about 25% when there is one male candidate but drops to about 5% when there are four male candidates.

In terms of the selection, higher levels of competition are associated with a lower probability that a woman is selected in both our full sample (diamond) and the women-inclusive contests sample (square). In the full model, the probability that a woman is selected is about 18.5% when there is only one male

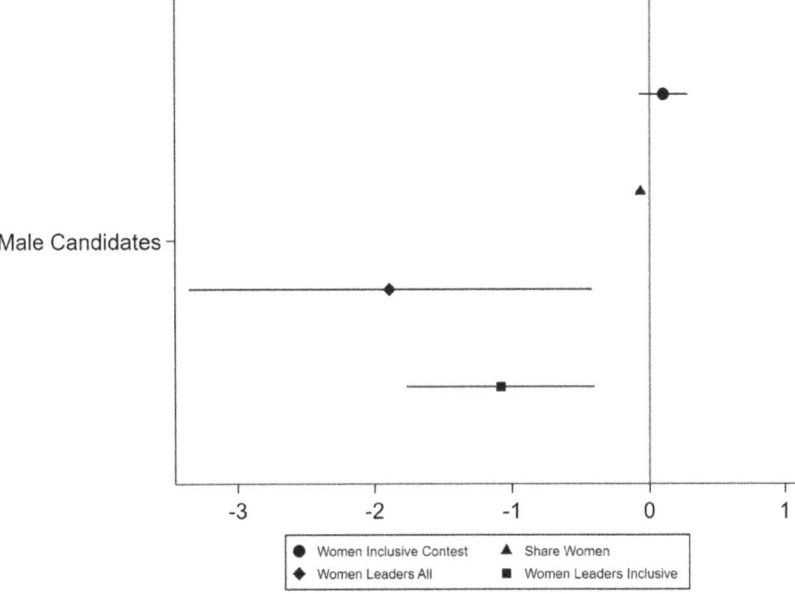

Figure 5 Election factors' effects on women's candidacy and selection.

Note: The coefficients and the standard errors (with 90% confidence intervals) come from the fully specified models, including our control variables.

candidate but it is virtually zero with more than two male candidates. In women-inclusive contests, the probability of a women leader decreases by 15% on average for every additional male candidate. While it is over 60% with only 1 male competitor, it falls to about 4% with five male candidates in the contest.

As we noted earlier, our data tells us that contests that include women are distinct from those that exclude them. One of the ways this manifests in the data is the absence of competition from men (and often other women) when women are candidates. In addition, the median number of candidates when women are selected as leaders is one in both our sample of all of the leadership contests and in the sample of women-inclusive contests. This means when women enter contests, there is very little competition from men. This supports the idea that whatever the conditions are that lead women to enter a contest, they may also be keeping men from entering or from making it past the initial screening stage. This is what the glass cliff theory would predict, where the opportunities taken by women are simply different than those taken by men (although with the caveat that we found very little and mostly opposite-than-expected performance effects on women's candidacy and selection). In contrast, the median number of candidates when men are selected is two in our full data and four in our women-inclusive sample. Thus, when men are present, women do not perform as well.

Culture Effects

Our last hypothesis (H3) posits that more women-friendly cultures should increase the likelihood of women running for party leadership and getting elected to the position. As we stated earlier, we test this hypothesis with a focus on party culture, measured by the share of women in the parliamentary party, the presence or absence of a voluntary party quota, and whether there has ever been a woman leader (or this leader is the first woman). We also account for the national parliamentary culture (whether the politics overall is more welcoming to women) by measuring the share of women in the national parliament at the time of the leadership election. We test each of these variables separately for each of our dependent variables. The results are presented in Figure 6 for the main independent variables, and the full models, with reporting of the control variables, are available in the online Appendix.

Figure 6 shows the share of women MPs in a party is a significant predictor of women's candidacy. It is positively and significantly associated with *inclusive leadership contests* (circle) and the *share of women candidates* (triangle). The probability of a women-inclusive leadership contest increases, on average, by about 3% for every 5% gain in the share of women MPs in the party. When the share of women is only 5%, this probability of inclusion is about 21%. When the share is 27% (the mean), the probability of inclusion is about 33%, and at parity, about 48%. For the share of women candidates, our model predicts about 25% of candidates will be women when their share of the parliamentary party is about 35% and about 33% when the share is 50%. Margin plots for these two models can be found in the online Appendix. On the other hand, for women leaders, it appears that the share of women MPs in the national parliament is more important for both models. In our full sample, the predicted probability of a woman getting elected as a leader is about 18.5% when our women in national parliament variable is at its mean (26%) but falls to about 9% at one standard deviation below this. In our inclusive sample, the probability of selecting a women leader is nearly 53% at the mean and falls to about 28% for one standard deviation below the mean. Our other culture variables, the presence of a party quota and having at least one previous leader are not significant in our models. The women MP results provide support for H3 for two out of four culture variables, where we predicted that gender-inclusive political culture increases the likelihood of women running for and getting elected as leaders.

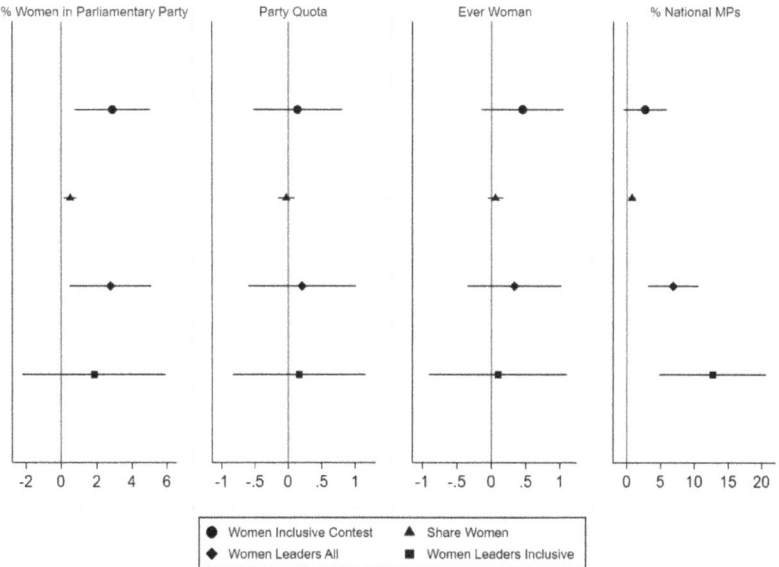

Figure 6 Cultural factors' effects on women's candidacy and selection.

Note: The coefficients and the standard errors (with 90% confidence intervals) come from the fully specified models with our control variables. Each of these measures of culture was included in a model on its own.

Gender Bias in Selection vs. Sample Selection Bias

With the models above, we tested how performance, selectorate, competition and culture affect women's likelihood of running and getting elected to party leadership. These results show that while some factors, like the selectorate type or the share of women in the parliamentary party, are significantly related to both women's entry into a leadership contest and their selection, many factors have heterogeneous effects across our four dependent variables. Thus, we have evidence to conclude that the factors determining the candidate pool may be different than those influencing the gender of the eventual leaders. However, because we have so many races that do not include any women, it's possible that our leader models suffer from sample selection bias. To investigate this, we now construct a selection model that links the process of women's inclusion as candidates to the outcome of the contest. These results are reported in Table 7. Not only does this allow us to test for the correlation of errors across models, but it also allows us to bring all our substantive variables into one model. We use a Heckman selection model, which requires that the selection equation includes at least one variable that is not included in the outcome equation. Based on the different conditions identified earlier for inclusion and selection, we construct our model to include performance resignations, member selection, and the party

Table 7 Heckman selection model

		(1) Baseline	(2) Controls
Second Stage: Leader Gender	Seat Change	0.470	0.641
		(0.511)	(0.526)
	Members	−0.368**	−0.459**
		(0.171)	(0.231)
	Male Candidates	−0.062**	−0.060**
		(0.027)	(0.032)
	Women in Parliament	1.118**	2.020***
		(0.486)	(0.752)
First Stage: Inclusive Contest	Only Performance Resignation	0.317*	0.348*
		(0.187)	(0.189)
	Members	0.755***	0.730***
		(0.211)	(0.218)
	Party Share of Women MPs	1.865***	1.647*
		(0.578)	(0.864)
	Observations (censored)	243(79)	243(79)
	ρ	0.219	−0.523
	Corr ρ	0.223	−0.581
	LR test of indep.	0.12	0.44
	$p > \chi^2$	0.727	0.508

Standard errors in parentheses
*** $p < 0.01$, ** $p < 0.05$, * $p < 0.1$

share of women for the first stage of having a women-inclusive contest. Then we use seat change to measure performance in the selection stage along with member selection, competition, and the national parliamentary share of women. Column one reports the baseline models while column two reports this model with the addition of all our control variables. The full reporting of this model is available in Table A.20.[17]

These models tell us two important pieces of information on women's candidacy and their selection as leaders. First, the results reported earlier hold in this specification. Performance resignations are a significant predictor of women's inclusion as well as member selection and the share of women in

---

[17] In these models we also chose to include member selection as the selectorate variable, given it was significant in both stages in separate analyses.

the parliamentary party. Women are more likely to be included in a leadership contest if the contest follows a performance resignation, includes selection by members, and there are more women in the party. For women leaders, member selection, competition, and overall parliamentary culture are more important in predicting women's fate once they are candidates. Member selection and competition are negatively related to women's selection while women's parliamentary representation is positively related to selection.

Second, the value reported for ρ, and the likelihood test tell us that the errors for these two processes are unrelated. So, while women must be in the pool to be chosen as leaders, the process of choosing the leader appears to be independent of the inclusion of women as candidates. We think this is an important and original conclusion. While this might seem counterintuitive, it makes sense to us given what we have shown of the data. In contests that include at least one woman, women are selected more often than men (60% women vs. 40% male in these 96 contests), 37.5% of these contests include no men at all, and 33.3% of these contests have no competition at all because there is only one candidate. Thus, we conclude that the important process to continue to explore and to emphasize as our contribution to the study of the selection of women leaders is to assess how women come to be included in the contest in the first place.

Moderating Effects

As our final set of analyses for candidacy and selection, we test the moderating effect hypotheses we set in the theory section. According to our H1b, we expect the performance effects to be especially strong in less gender-inclusive systems. And, we expect the positive effects of an exclusive selectorate on women's elections to leadership to be particularly strong and the negative effects of an inclusive selectorate to be weaker if there is a performance downturn (H2a) and in more women-friendly environments (H2b).

To test the conditioning effects of political culture (H1b and H2b), we focus on the share of women MPs in the party for the candidacy models and the share of women MPs in the parliament for the selection models. We also use the party culture variable of whether the party ever had a woman leader to identify whether women candidates experience different conditions when there has previously been a woman leader. In addition, to test our H2a (the moderating effects of party performance for the relationship between selectorate and women's candidacy and leadership), we test for the interactive effect of seat change. Our models also include all the control variables from before.

Table A.21 in the online Appendix reports the results for all our interactions with the party share of women and our substantive variables. We only report

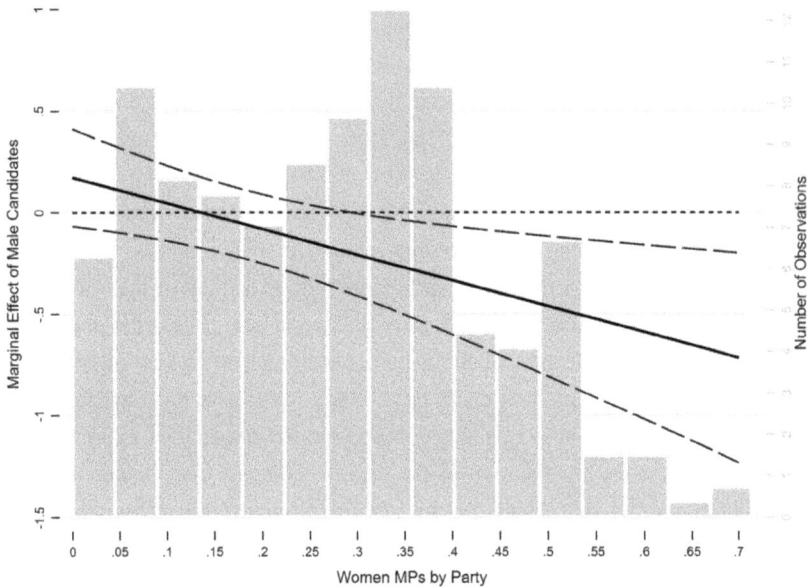

Figure 7 Party share of women MPs and male candidates.

Note: The margins and the standard errors (with 90% confidence intervals) come from the fully specified models with our control variables and interactions.

the significant results here. As can be seen, the only significant conditioning effects were for the government loss variable for just one DV and for the male candidates variable.

Figure 7 reports the marginal effect of the number of male candidates conditioned by the number of women MPs in the party. We see that the number of candidates has a negative effect on women's candidacy as the party share of women MPs increases. For example, the change in the predicted probability of seeing a women-inclusive contest when there is one versus four male candidates is about −3.7% when the share of women is one standard deviation below the mean. However, it is nearly −12% when the share of women MPs is at its mean (27%). Thus, the number of candidates becomes increasingly detrimental to women's candidacy as party equality increases.

In Figure 8, the interaction between having a previous woman leader and government loss is negative and significant. While losing the government or having a previous woman leader does not have a significant impact on the likelihood of seeing a women-inclusive contest, if they are present at the same time (i.e. a party that has had a previous woman leader and just lost the government), then the likelihood of an inclusive contest decreases by about 4%. This is an interesting finding, suggesting that the glass cliff theory of performance downturn increasing the likelihood of women's candidacy only works if there was

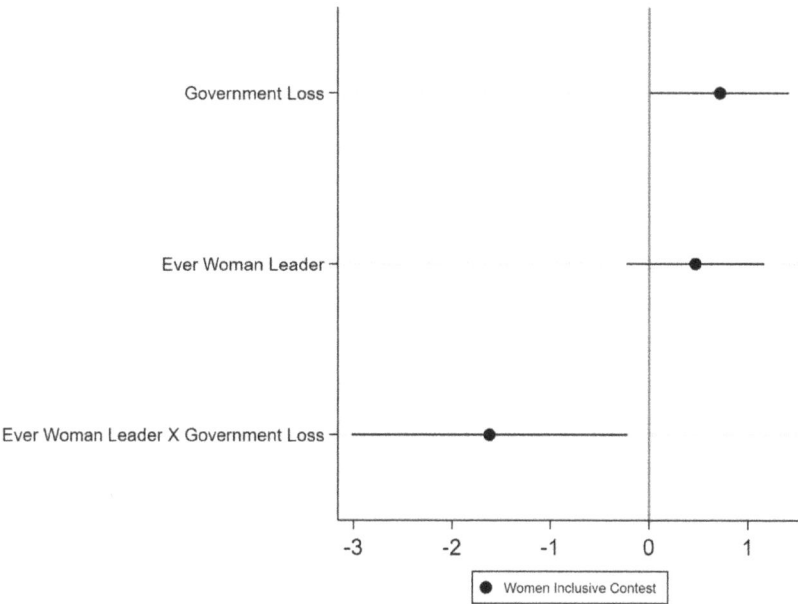

Figure 8 Previous women leaders and government loss.

Note: The margins and the standard errors (with 90% confidence intervals) come from the fully specified models with our control variables and interactions.

no woman leader in the past (the culture was not inclusive). Once there is a woman leader, glass cliff stops working.

We also test the same interaction effects on the likelihood of a woman becoming the leader. In these models, instead of using women's share of the party MPs, we include women's share of the parliament (following the previous results). The only significant interaction variable is the ever-woman and male candidates interaction.[18]

Figure 9 reports the interaction of ever-woman and the number of male candidates. While competition has a negative effect when there is no previous woman leader, this effect is even greater when there is one. The predicted probability of a woman leader winning an inclusive contest when there is one male candidate with no previous woman leader is about 66% but decreases at a steady rate as more men enter the contest to about 35% with four candidates. If there was previously a woman leader, this probability starts lower, at about 49% when

---

[18] Parliamentary share of women MPs and seat changes also produce statistically significant interactions with the male candidates variable, but for the observed values of the parliamentary share and seat change variables in our data, there are no conditioning effects, and therefore, we do not report those results in the text.

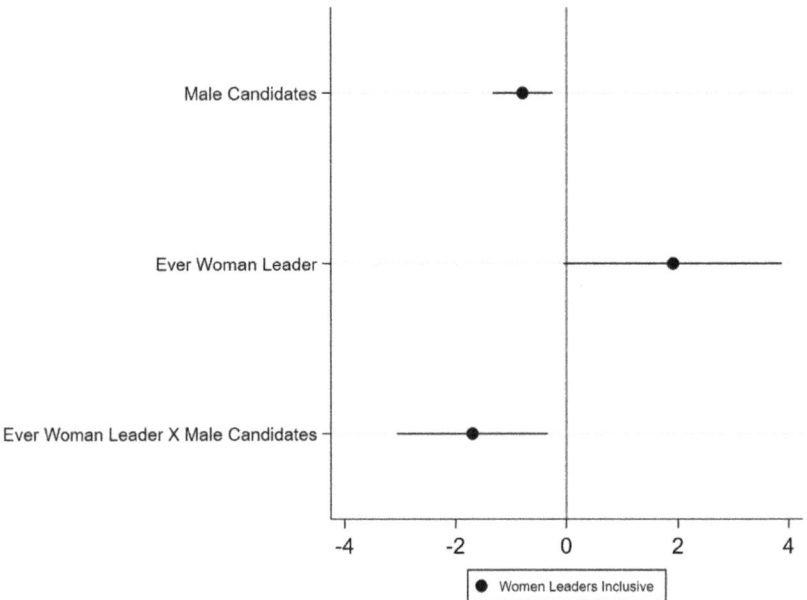

Figure 9 Previous woman leader and male candidates.

Note: The margins and the standard errors (with 90% confidence intervals) come from the fully specified models with our control variables and interactions.

there is one male candidate, but decreases much faster to about less than 2% when there are four.[19]

Overall, then, while these conditioning effects provide us with interesting information, we do not find any support for our conditioning hypotheses. Interestingly, while we found that women are more likely to run for and get elected to leadership positions in women-inclusive cultures, we see with the results in this section that women-inclusive cultures may become more detrimental for women when a party lost office and when there are more men running in leadership elections. We speculate that this may be because parties in more women-friendly cultures may feel less pressure to protect women and push for them compared to less inclusive cultures.

Conclusion

The analysis of our data has highlighted interesting patterns in both women's inclusion in the candidate pool for party leadership and their success in becoming leaders. In this section, we first argued that internal electoral politics may not follow the gendered patterns we find in legislative or executive elections.

---

[19] Predicted probabilities for women leaders for these models can be found in Table A.23.

Internal party elections for leadership are a higher-information environment where many of the personal barriers that women face in the decision to run for office have already been overcome. Thus, decisions to pursue party leadership among women should be less gendered than the decision to run for electoral office. Instead, women are likely strategic in their choice to pursue party leadership and become candidates when the opportunity is right. Yet, despite this rather positive note, we noted that we see very few women candidates and very few women leaders in advanced democracies and went on to explore why this has been the case.

By examining the effects of performance, election details, and the gender inclusiveness of political culture on both women's candidacy and selection for leadership, we found that women's inclusion in leadership contests is associated with a variety of conditions that structure party leadership change. These include leadership changes that occur after performance resignations, when leadership elections are inclusive, and when women are well represented in the parliamentary party.

We also present interesting data on how women and men compete for leadership, showing that women's inclusiveness is often accompanied by men's absence, further supporting our theoretical argument that party leadership change is gendered. On a positive note, we show that when women become candidates, they often face little competition and thus have a high probability of becoming leaders. However, we also show that there are still many more contests that don't include any women at all. In terms of women's success in gaining leadership, we show that this competition and women's descriptive representation in parliament are most important. Thus, our overarching conclusion, and one major contribution to the study of women's leadership, highlights the importance of women's inclusion as leadership candidates. Because we are able to provide evidence determining what party performance, organization, and gender-inclusive culture conditions encourage women to contest leadership elections, we are able to contribute to the growing literature on women's opportunities within political parties and their pathways to power leadership positions. We also push the literature forward by illuminating how exploring the process (women's candidacy) in addition to focusing on the outcome (women leaders) can reveal important patterns in the gendered nature of political careers.

4 Tenure of Women Party Leaders

On September 6, 2022, Liz Truss became the leader of the UK Conservative Party, joining Margaret Thatcher and Theresa May as the only women ever to hold this post. She rose to leadership following Boris Johnson's resignation. Although Boris Johnson's tenure was riddled with scandals, he served three years in the position. In contrast, Liz Truss resigned after only six weeks following a tax plan that called into question her competency and ability to carry out her mandate. Truss left office after one failed policy, while Johnson was allowed to maintain his leadership through numerous party crises. "Teflon" Johnson withstood at least three major party crises before his departure.[20] He was accused of hosting Downing Street parties that flouted COVID-19 lockdown rules. He even faced criminal penalties in April 2021 for breaking his own rules on multiple occasions.[21] This finally motivated a group of MPs to call for a confidence vote within the party, but Johnson survived with 59% of Conservative MPs supporting him.[22,23] He finally resigned in July, after a sexual harassment scandal involving a Tory MP, followed by definitive proof that Johnson had lied to his party about his knowledge of the harassment.[24]

In contrast to Johnson's ability to withstand so much turmoil, Liz Truss resigned as party leader after only six weeks and one particularly problematic policy move. After introducing an economic plan that would cut taxes without providing an alternative source of government funding, her unpopularity in public rose to levels that even Johnson did not experience immediately before he resigned.[25] Facing severe public backlash, the resignation of her home secretary, and fifteen MPs calling for her to resign, she resigned, stating she could no longer deliver on the mandate for which she was elected.[26] It was as if Liz truss was on quicksand upon getting the leadership position: it quickly pulled her inside and sank her leadership to a point of no return within only a few weeks. Johnson's leadership, on the other hand, was on cement: no matter what he did, he did not sink, and only after too many blows did the cement finally give way.

These rather starkly different standards for women versus men leaders are not unique to the United Kingdom either. In recent years, Sanna Marin, the leader of the Finnish Social Democrats and the Finnish Prime Minister between 2020 and 2023, and Jacinda Arden, the leader of the New Zealand Labour

---

[20] This is the nickname given to Johnson for his ability to withstand many scandals (*The Week* September 6, 2022, accessed 11/2/2022)

[21] *The Guardian* April 12 2022, accessed 11/2/2022.

[22] For perspective, the majority of Tory confidence votes called since 1970 have been against the women leaders, Thatcher and May (3 of 5).

[23] *The Guardian* June 6 2022, accessed 11/2/2022.

[24] *The Week* September 6, 2022, accessed 11/2/2022.

[25] *The Guardian* October 1, 2022, accessed 11/2/2022.

[26] *The Guardian* October 20 2022 accessed 11/3/2022; *The New York Times* October 20 2022. accessed 11/3/2022.

Party and the country's Prime Minister between 2017 and 2023, were dogged by sexist remarks from reporters, online commentators, and fellow politicians. Sanna Marin was labeled as unfit for office for drinking and dancing at a private party,[27] while Tucker Carlson on Fox News referred to Jacinda Arden as the "lady with the big teeth" when discussing her resignation from party leadership.[28] Both leaders had relatively short tenures as their parties' leaders.

If the leadership positions are glass ceilings that are hard for women to shatter and win, their survival in the post is like standing on quicksand where any move can agitate the sand and sink them deeper to a point of no return. In this section, we unpack leaders' tenure and their removal from office and test whether women leaders' performances in office, their selectorates, leadership election details, and the political culture affect their tenure differently than men's. Our results suggest that performance failures, especially seat losses, have particularly detrimental effects on women, and seat gains significantly help women more than men. Leader election details, particularly the inclusiveness of the selectorate (whether membership or delegates elect the leader) and the number of candidates, also affect women's tenures differently than men's. The smaller the number of candidates, the better the elected leaders survive, potentially because smaller candidate numbers suggest the unwillingness of others to run for party leadership – perhaps due to the party's standing. Interestingly, we find that the gender-inclusiveness of political culture does not affect women's tenure any differently than men's. We discuss our results and potential explanations for these results in the rest of the section.

Women's Tenure in Office

Previous research has provided mixed conclusions on the longevity of women's tenure in political leadership. Empirical evidence suggests women in leadership posts last longer than men (Berlinski, Dewan, and Dowding 2007), have similar tenures (Cross and Blais 2012), or spend less time in these positions (O'Neill, Pruysers, and Stewart 2021). As we discussed in Section 2, our Party Leaders Dataset shows that women leaders appear to have similar lengths of tenure in office compared to men, but we argue that factors that affect leader tenure may have stronger effects on women leaders than men.

Party members and elites hold different perceptions of the leadership qualities and leadership styles of women (Holman, Merolla, and Zechmeister 2011; O'Brien 2015; Perdue 2016; Yates 2019). Differences in the way party members judge their leaders may be the result of outright gender bias or stem from

---

[27] *Glamour Magazine* August 25 2022, accessed 09/07/2023.
[28] *Washington Post* January 19 2023, accessed 09/07/2023.

stereotypical beliefs about when and how women are best suited to excel in leadership positions. Men can be offered the benefit of the doubt in tough situations because they are seen as natural leaders. They are often perceived as assertive and self-confident when exercising power, while women in similar situations are perceived as hostile (at best) and irrational (at worst). When women exercise stereotypical feminine leadership, showing compassion and empathy, they are viewed as weak and compromising or incompetent (for an in-depth discussion, see Holman, Merolla, and Zechmeister 2011). All this can open women up to more direct challenges under various conditions where men would typically be isolated from such contestation.

Women leaders, therefore, often find themselves navigating a precarious political landscape, akin to standing on *quicksand*, where their performance, the details of their election, and the overall political culture toward women's leadership can jeopardize their position. Unlike men, who can enjoy more resilience in leadership roles, women often face heightened scrutiny. The challenges they encounter are multifaceted, ranging from the gender biases we described earlier, to unrealistic expectations, negative legitimacy evaluations, and skepticism about their mandate. The quicksand they stand on can be easily agitated by any downturns, biases, or negative legitimacy/competence evaluations, potentially resulting in shorter tenures for women.

Performance Effects

The literature on party leaders' tenure in office points to leader performance as the most crucial factor in determining the length of tenure. Most recently, Somer-Topcu and Weitzel (2023) show, with the same Party Leaders Dataset, that weak electoral performance and government loss are the most important factors for leader replacements. Previous work by Andrews and Jackman (2008) and Ennser-Jedenastik and Schumacher (2015), focusing on Westminster systems and Austria, respectively, also presents evidence that electoral performance is the most crucial factor affecting leader duration in office, and Bille (1997) and Ennser-Jedenastik and Müller (2015) show that loss of government increases the likelihood of leader replacements. In addition to election performance and government status, we also argue that losses in the opinion polls also increase the risk of getting replaced.

How do these performance indicators affect women and men differently? O'Brien (2015), with an analysis of eleven democracies between the 1960s and 2013, shows that changes in party seat share have significantly different effects for women versus men in party leadership positions. Women's tenure is more likely to be cut short when they lose seats (compared to men). Building on O'Brien's influential work, we expect performance downturns to have larger negative effects on women leaders' tenure. The stereotypes of women not being as qualified as men for leadership or not having the qualities of effective leaders suggest that any performance declines under a woman's leadership would be perceived as the leader's failure, forcing the woman leader to resign quicker than a man would. We expect patience to run shorter for women when they are performing weakly; hence, the likelihood of replacement increases when party performance declines. Taking O'Brien's results forward, we argue that *any* performance downturn, whether it is losing seat shares, government position, or polling standing, more negatively affects women's tenure compared to men's. We also argue that the negative effects should be exacerbated if the woman leader experiences a major loss (a very high seat share loss and/or government loss combined with high seat share loss) and dissipate if the woman leader helps the party increase the party seat share significantly and gain office.

While losses are more detrimental for women compared to men, we argue, similar to O'Brien (2015) that performance gains should be particularly helpful to women compared to men. O'Brien (2015) shows that when parties led by a woman win seats, the leaders are more likely to stay in office. She argues that because women face challenges to become leaders, only the most competent women rise up to the position of party leadership and enjoy a performance advantage when they win seats. We test this hypothesis in a setting where we have an extended list of woman leaders and multiple performance indicators beyond only seat gains.

Our first hypothesis, therefore, is as follows:

> *H1: Party performance likely has a greater impact on women's tenure, both when parties experience losses (greater negative impact compared to men) and when parties experience gains (greater positive impact compared to men), and these effects likely intensify for major losses/gains.*

Leadership Election Details

Performance, while crucial, is not the only factor that affects leader tenure. We also argue that the *selection process*, especially the inclusiveness of the selection process, and the details of the leadership election can affect the legitimacy of a leader's power.

Cozza and Somer-Topcu (2021) and Cozza, Di Landro, and Somer-Topcu (2023) show that inclusive selection processes, especially membership votes for party leadership elections, positively affect the legitimacy evaluations of the selection procedure and the elected leaders. Following this argument, we argue that when the selectorate is small and exclusively composed of party elites, whether it is the parliamentary delegation or the party executive, the choice of leader may be viewed as an elite-based and indirect mandate lacking political legitimacy. If a leader did not secure a large following within the party, their ability to make the tough decisions necessary to lead a party through poor electoral performance, a public image crisis, or scandal, for example, may be more limited and illicit greater pushback.

While we expect these negative legitimacy effects of small and exclusive elite selectorates to negatively affect all leaders' tenure, we also expect these effects of selectorates to be larger for women for two reasons. First, women, who face explicit or implicit biases against their leadership, typically have to forge broader coalitions to support their leadership in office. When a small group of party elites appoints a woman to party leadership, this broad consensus support would be lacking and difficult to establish. In turn, any mistakes, small or large, would be more likely to end the woman's tenure.

Second, an inclusive and larger electorate selecting a woman would grant *higher* legitimacy to the woman leader (see, e.g., Aldrich et al. 2023). We know from the literature and from our findings in Section 3 that getting elected the party leader is more difficult for women when a large and inclusive electorate of party members is involved with the selection (Fox and Oxley 2003; Rahat and Hazan 2010). Women, who are elected via an inclusive and large selectorate can do so only by overcoming the biases of these larger masses. We argue that when they can do that and win in these more difficult races, they can claim a larger mandate and are likely seen as more competent and legitimate compared to men. In contrast, those women who are appointed as party leaders by a small group of party elites are likely seen as less deserving and more placeholders. Therefore, we expect the negative (positive) effects of small (large) selectorates on tenure to be higher for women leaders. Following our earlier argument on the detrimental (uplifting) effects of performance downturns (upticks), we also argue that these positive effects of inclusive selectorates can intensify when the woman leader experiences performance downturns or upticks.[29]

Hence, our selectorate hypotheses are as follows:

> *H2: The tenure of women leaders is likely longer (shorter) compared to men, the larger and more inclusive (smaller and less inclusive) the selectorate for leadership.*

---

[29] At the same time, we acknowledge that our expectations go against the canonical selectorate theory of Bueno de Mesquita et al. (2002), which argues that smaller selectorates are easier to placate with private goods while in office that should help with leader tenure. However, in this age of presidentialization of party politics and the media dominance of politics, we argue that the positive legitimacy effects of membership elections likely have bigger effects on leader performance and tenure.

H2a: The positive effects of the inclusive selectorate selection process likely dissipate (strengthen) when there is a performance downturn (uptick).

In addition to the selectorate structure, we also explore whether leadership competition details play a role in leadership survival, particularly the number of candidates and the margin of victory in the leadership election. A crowded slate of candidates for the leadership post may provide information to party elites or members about the desirability of the post, and the winner of such a competitive election can claim a higher mandate. In addition, following the work of Cozza, Di Landro, and Somer-Topcu (2023), we argue that when more candidates run for party leadership, each must put more effort into winning the hearts and minds of the selectorate, showcasing their qualities and competence. Therefore, as the number of candidates increases, we expect higher legitimacy evaluations for the winner. Similarly, a high margin of victory would allow the elected leader to claim a larger mandate, helping the winner to solidify their position in office. Therefore, we expect a leader who wins the leadership election in a crowded slate and with a high margin of victory to be able to claim a stronger mandate, which in turn should strengthen their leadership position and help them survive longer in office with that mandate.

Once again, we expect gendered effects of leadership election details. Facing a high number of candidates and winning the election with a large margin of victory likely convey information about women candidates that dispels stereotypes about their suitability for that position. Defeating a large number of competitors and winning decisively can help voters infer that the elected woman is particularly high quality and deserves the position, helping her strongly establish her leadership position, dispel attacks against her leadership, and achieve a strong grip on the leadership position that may help her stay in the office longer.

At the same time, similar to the selectorate effects, we expect performance in leadership to condition the effects of leader election details. We expect the positive effects of the higher number of candidates and the higher margin of victory to improve during performance upticks and dampen during performance downturns. Our leadership election details hypotheses then are as follows:

H3: Women likely have longer (shorter) tenures than men when they are elected in leadership elections with a large (small) number of candidates and higher (lower) margins of victory.

H3a: These positive effects of election details on women's tenure likely weaken (strengthen) when the leader performs poorly (well).

Political Culture Effects

Finally, we expect that women's removal will be linked with overall gender equality and inclusiveness in political parties and in the broader political system. In parties with previous women leaders and higher shares of women MPs, we expect the gender differences in leader tenure to be less pronounced, all else being equal. Therefore, we expect women's tenure to be less likely to be any different from men's tenure in women-friendly parties and parliaments, while women should have shorter tenures compared to men in less friendly contexts (H4). We also expect the gender dynamics that we have hypothesized so far, regarding performance, selectorate, and election details, to be especially strong in systems with smaller levels of women's representation in the party and parliamentary politics, where the biases against women in politics are more paramount, and women are not seen as natural political leaders. Our final set of hypotheses is as follows:

> *H4: Gendered differences in leader tenures are more (less) likely to occur in less (more) women-friendly parties and parliaments.*
>
> *H4a: The gendered tenure differences due to performance, selectorate, and leadership election details are more (less) likely to occur in systems with less (more) women representation in politics.*

Research Design

The dependent variable for the duration models is the time (in months) a leader is in office. We measure a leader's tenure from the month of her official appointment to the month of her resignation date. An important point is that the leaders do not necessarily resign in the same month as the new leader's appointment. It may take months to fill the position after the resignation announcement. Therefore, given that our goal is to understand why leaders resign, it is important that we use the effective resignation date and not the new leader's appointment date to mark the end of a leader's tenure. Our dataset codes both the resignation and appointment dates, and we rely on the former to code the end of leaders' tenure.

We use Cox duration models with a robust variance estimator to examine the factors determining leaders' durations in office. The Cox proportional hazard model does not require a specification of an underlying hazard rate shape, as parametric models do (Alt and King 1994; Warwick 1992). We censor all months for the leaders that are still in office at the end of the time period of PLD, all leaders who were appointed before the start of our data period, all the interim leaders' periods in office, the periods between the resignation of the old leader and the appointment date of the new leader, and the two leaders in our data who died in office (John Smith of the UK Labour Party and Jack Layton of the Canadian New Democracy).

To test the performance effects and, similar to Section 3, we use change in seat share, loss of government, and polling status compared to the last election result to measure our performance variables. We do not use the qualitative performance resignation variable here, since this information enters the data only after a resignation occurs. Similar to Section 3, we run our models separately by including and excluding the polling change variable. In Hypothesis 1, we also argue that major losses (gains) should harm (help) women more than men. In Section 3, we defined a major loss (gain) in two ways: (1) losing (gaining) more than 10% of the seat share, and (2) losing (gaining) more than 10% of the seat share and losing (gaining) the government status at the same time.

We then move to the leadership selection details to examine how the appointment details affect leader tenure. We code *Inclusive Selectorate* 1 if a party chooses its leader through a vote of rank-and-file members or through the party delegates' votes at a party conference. As opposed to the previous section's design, we opted not to differentiate membership and delegate elections in this section, given that we have very few women who are elected through membership vote once the last leaders still in office as of 2020 are excluded due to the survival data modeling requirements. To test how the leadership election details affect women leaders' duration in office compared to men's, we use two variables. The *Number of Candidates* codes the total number of candidates who ran in the first (or the only) round of the leadership election.[30] The *Margin of Victory* codes the vote difference between the top two candidates in the first round (or the vote share of the only candidate if there was only one candidate).[31]

Finally, to test H4 and H4a, we examine how the broader political culture toward women affects women leaders' tenure (H4) and conditions the effects of the other variables (H4a). We use the same four measures for the gender-inclusive political culture as in Section 3: (1) a binary measure for whether a party has ever had a women leader, *Ever Woman*; (2) *Party Share of Women MPs*, the share of women in the parliamentary party; (3) *Women in Parliament*, which codes the share of women MPs in the national parliament; and (4) *Party Gender Quota*, a binary variable coded 1 starting in the year the party

---

[30] Our focus in Section 3 was on the share of men candidates rather than the raw number of candidates. However, because we are interested in how the incumbent leader's election details affect their survival and we use all leaders in the models, we use the raw number of candidates in this section.
[31] We did not include the *Margin of Victory* variable in our models in Section 3 because the leadership election results come at the end of the leader selection process and cannot affect the decision to run for or the ability to win the leadership positions.

introduced a gender quota. While we test the effects of all these four variables on women's tenure compared to men's to test our Hypothesis 4, due to theoretical reasons and high correlation between some of these variables, we only use the *Ever Woman* and *Party Share of Women MPs* in the models where we include the cultural variables as control variables. Theoretically, we expect that having a woman leader in the past and the current share of women MPs should reflect the party's inclusivity better than the overall parliamentary culture and the gender quotas. Parliamentary culture shows inclusivity across parties but should not have strong direct effects on leader tenure in a particular party, and gender quotas likely help women only through their effects of increasing the number of women MPs.

We test the conditioning effects of performance (H2a and H3a) and political culture (H4a) by running triple interaction models between our key variables, gender dummy variable, and the seat share change (for H2a and H3a), and the party shares of women MPs (for H4a). While triple interactions are hard to interpret, the split sample approach makes it difficult to make any inferences about the statistical differences across models, when we have small numbers of women leaders in the dataset.

Our models also include several control variables that have been shown to have significant and substantive effects on leader tenure. First, we control for leader age (*Leader Age*) in the models because we expect older leaders to be more likely to be replaced (Andrews and Jackman 2008; Cross and Blais 2012; O'Brien 2015), given that they are closer to retirement and often parties go after young blood to energize the party base. Second, we add a dummy variable for whether the party was in government because incumbent parties are unlikely to replace their leaders while in office (*In Government*). We again use a variable for left parties (*Left Party*) that is coded 1 for the social democratic, green, and left libertarian parties in our dataset. As we showed in our data section, left parties are more likely to appoint women leaders, and hence, we expect them to be more supportive of women leaders once they are in office. Fourth, we add a dummy variable for the leader-centric countries, Australia, Canada, Germany, Ireland, New Zealand, and the United Kingdom, where the party leaders are more forefront compared to many PR systems in Europe (*Leader-Centric*), where leader tenure is likely shaped by different considerations than in more party-centric systems. In addition, as we show later, the only variable that appears to have significantly different effects for women and men when we run the full models separately for women and men is this leader-centric systems variable. In Figure 12, we see that women have significantly less risk of failing in office in leader-centric systems. Therefore, we also include the interaction of leader-centric systems and the gender variable as a control to all models (*Leader-Centric X Woman*). Finally, we add a dummy variable, coded 1 for the 2000s and 2010s, given that leader tenures have shortened in recent decades (*2000s and 2010s*).

Results

Before we test our hypotheses on the gendered effects of performance, selectorate, election details, and political culture on tenure, we first show how these variables affect leader tenure more generally by pooling all leaders together.[32] Figure 10 shows the Cox proportional hazard model coefficients, where the coefficients of this model represent the risk of experiencing a leadership replacement event, that is, the likelihood of failure. Hence, a negative coefficient would indicate a decrease in the risk of a leader replacement, while

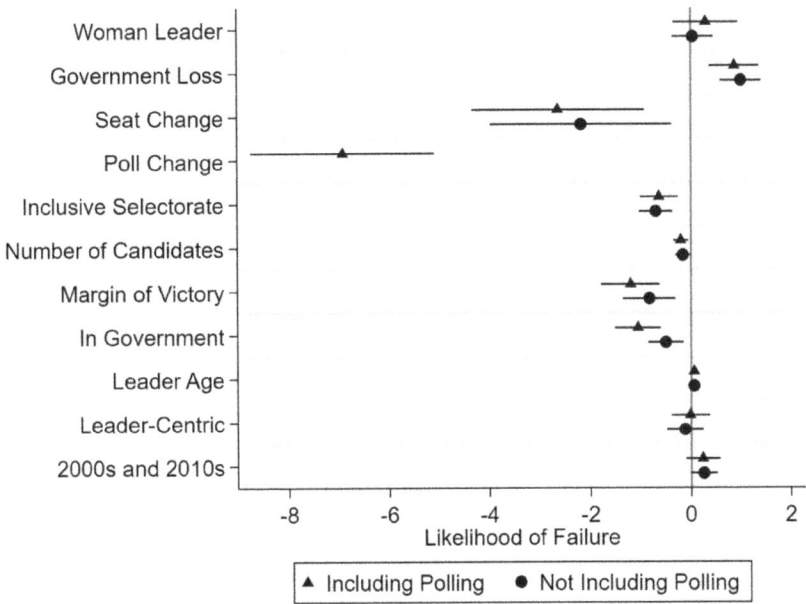

Figure 10 All leaders pooled: Factors that affect leader tenure.

Note: The coefficients and the standard errors (with 90% confidence intervals) come from the fully specified model pooling all leaders together (see the online Appendix for the full results). Two separate models' results are presented. The triangles show the results from the Cox proportional hazard model that includes the polling change variable (N = 8,435), and the circles show the results from the model excluding the polling change variable (N = 12,514).

---

[32] In the online Appendix, we present the full model outcomes for all the results we present in this section.

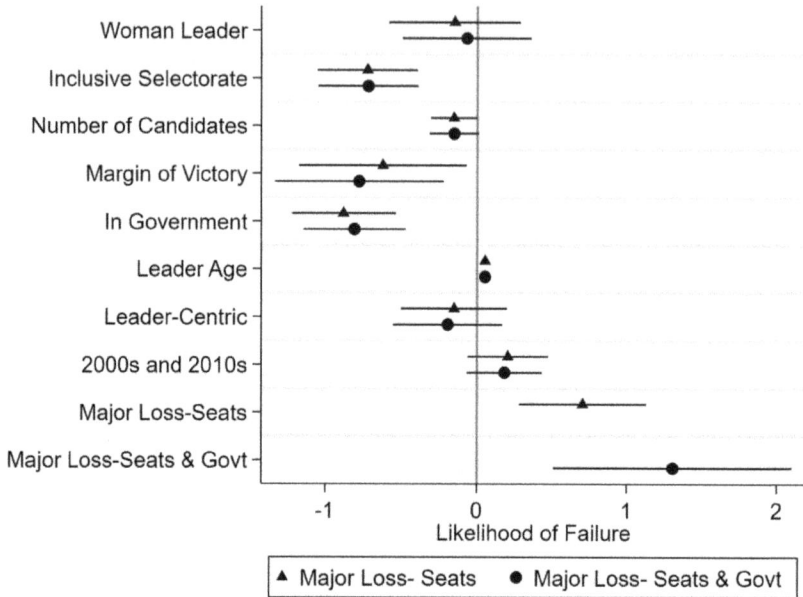

Figure 11 All leaders pooled: Factors that affect leader tenure – using major loss.

Note: The coefficients and the standard errors (with 90% confidence intervals) come from the fully specified model pooling all leaders together (see the online Appendix for the full results). Two separate models' results are presented. The triangles show the results using the major loss variable defined as losing more than 10% of the seats, and the circles show the results with the major loss defined as losing more than 10% of the seats and the government status.

a positive coefficient would mean a higher risk of a leader replacement.[33] We report the results of two models in this figure: one with the change in the polling standing variable included and one without this variable due to the loss of a large number of observations when we include the polling data. We note, however, that all variables show similar effects across these two models. Next, in Figure 11, we show the same pooled results, but instead of seat change and government loss we use the two major loss variables: (1) 10% or more seat losses, and (2) 10% or more seat losses and government loss.

To start with the most important variable, *Woman Leader*, we do not see any statistically significant difference between women and men leaders across these two figures (the coefficients are not statistically significantly different from 0). This is consistent with our data that the average duration of women

---

[33] We note that this pooled model does not include the two political culture variables and the left party dummy because, theoretically, we would not expect these variables to affect leader tenure for the pooled data of both men and women leaders.

and men in office is very similar. The results in Figure 10 show that losing seats results in shorter tenures. The negative coefficient suggests that seat losses (negative seat changes) significantly increase the likelihood of failure for party leaders. The hazard ratio for the seat change is 0.113, which suggests that if a party loses about 10% of its seats, the risk of failing for the leader increases by about 8.9%. The government loss variable is also statistically significant and positive and tells us that leaders are more likely to lose office when they lose the government. The hazard ratio for government loss is 2.68, meaning that a leader who costs the party the office is about 2.7 times more likely to fail. The polling performance has a substantively larger effect. The coefficient suggests that a negative change in the party's polling standing is more likely to cost the party leader her office. The results mean that a 1% loss in the polling standing compared to the previous election result increases the likelihood of failure by about 10%. Moving to the two major loss dummy variables in Figure 11, we see that both cause an increased likelihood of failure for leaders, although the second version, which codes the major loss as 10% or more seat losses and government loss, shows stronger negative effects on tenure. The hazard ratio of 3.7 for the second major loss variable means that a leader who costs the party more than 10% of its seats and the government is 3.7 times more likely to lose their position.

The negative and significant coefficients for the selectorate inclusiveness, number of candidates, and margin of victory across the two figures suggest that leaders who are elected with membership or delegate votes, in crowded slates, and with a high margin of victory are more likely to survive longer in office (the likelihood of failure is negative), findings that are consistent with our hypotheses and the argument that these election details help improve leader legitimacy and increase their mandate, as argued by Cozza, Di Landro, and Somer-Topcu (2023).

The control variables also work as expected: parties are less likely to replace their leaders when they are in office, and older leaders are more likely to be replaced. Being a leader-centric country, however, does not seem to affect leader tenure, on average, and while leaders appear to have shorter tenures in the 2000s and 2010s (the likelihood of failure is larger), there is not a statistically significant difference across time.

Next, we test the effects of all variables on women and men separately before we turn to the interaction effects to directly test our hypotheses. The coefficient graphs in Figure 12 and Figure 13 show the separate effects of the variables for women and men leaders, first for the seat change, government loss, and polling variables (in two separate models in Figure 12, due to significant drop in N with polling change), and second for the major loss variable that combined more

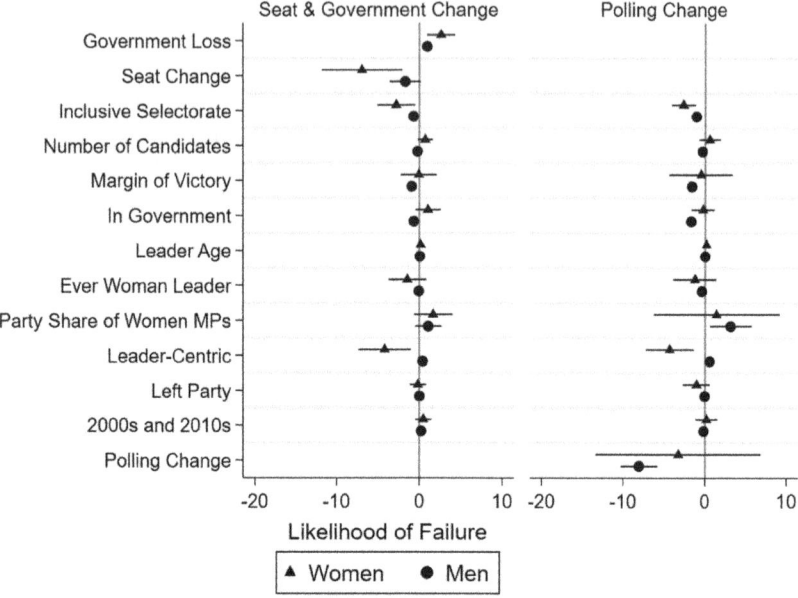

Figure 12 Factors that separately affect the tenures of women and men leaders.

Note: The coefficients and the standard errors (with 90% confidence intervals) come from the fully specified models run separately for women (triangles) and men (circles) leaders. The left-side graph shows the effects of seat change and government change and the right-side graph shows the effect of polling change along with the effects of the other variables.

than 10% seat loss with government loss. We note that due to the low number of women leaders in the dataset, the women-only model shows larger standard errors, which increases the likelihood of confidence interval overlapping across women and men. Therefore, none of the variables appear to be statistically different for women and men, except the number of candidates variable in Figure 13 and the leader-centric dummy variable in both figures. The coefficient for the number of candidates variable shows that women have a higher likelihood of failure when there is competition for the position, while men have a lower likelihood, and the hazard ratios suggest that women are 1.6 times more likely to fail for each additional candidate, while each additional candidate reduces the likelihood of failure by about 22% for men. This is against our expectations. We test whether the results change when we interact the variables with the gender dummy later. The Leader-Centric variable results posit that women have a lower likelihood of failure in the more leader-centric countries of Australia, Canada, Germany, New Zealand, and the UK, compared to party-centric countries. We tested whether this significant difference is because

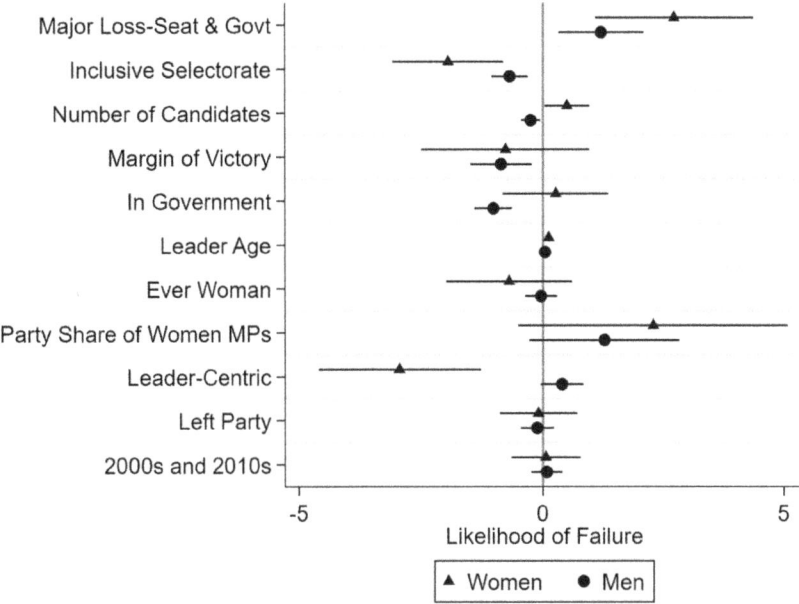

Figure 13 Factors that separately affect the tenures of women and men leaders – using major loss.

Note: The coefficients and the standard errors (with 90% confidence intervals) come from the two fully specified models run separately for women (triangles) and men (circles) leaders with a focus on the major loss variable along with the other variables. The major loss variable here is defined as losing more than 10% of the seats and losing the government status.

of Angela Merkel's long tenure, but the results stayed robust when we dropped Merkel's leadership from the data. Because of this latter finding, going forward, our models include the leader-centric dummy variable and its interaction with the woman leader dummy variable as control variables. None of the other variables show any statistical difference for women and men across these three models, but testing the hypotheses requires interacting these variables with the Woman Leader variable, to which we turn now.

Performance Effects

Moving to test the interaction effects, our performance hypothesis (H1) states that women should be punished more for performance downturns than men, especially for major losses, and that performance improvements should help women stay in office longer compared to men. In Figure 14, we test the effects of changes in seats, government status, and polling on women and men leaders by interacting the variables with the gender of the party leader, and we test the effects of major loss variables interacted with the gender dummy in Figure 15.

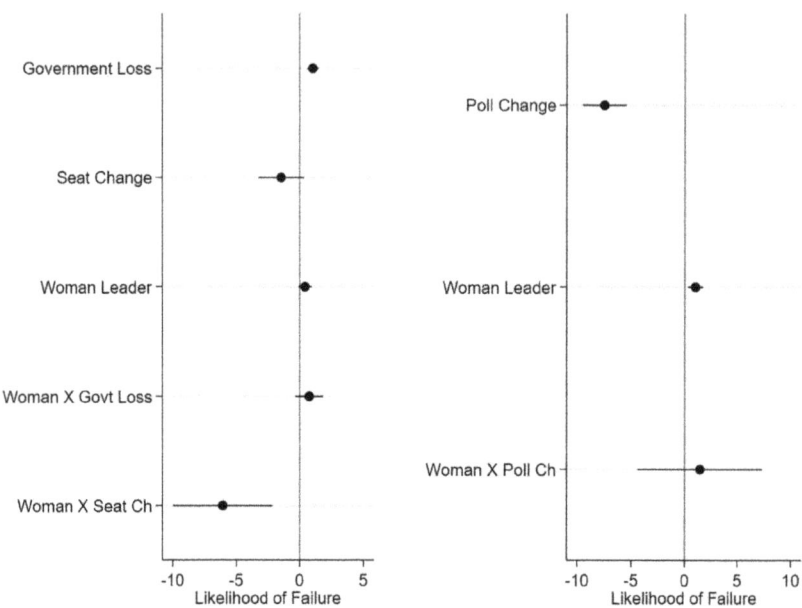

Figure 14 Performance effects on leader tenures – seat change, government status, polling.

Note: The coefficients and the standard errors (with 90% confidence intervals) come from the fully specified interaction models. The left-side graph shows the effects of seat change and government change and the right-side graph shows the effect of polling change along with the effects of the other variables.

All models also include all the control variables.[34] If performance downturns and improvements have stronger negative and positive effects (respectively) on women's tenure, as expected, we should see negative and statistically significant interaction coefficients for the *Seat Change* and *Polling Change* variables, indicating that seat losses and polling downturns increase the likelihood of failure for women, and gains help them stay in office longer. Government Loss in Figure 14 and the Major Loss variables in Figure 15 should, on the other hand, have a positive interaction effect, suggesting that women are more likely to lose their leadership positions when they cost the party government status or caused a major loss.

Figure 14 shows that seat change indeed has stronger negative effects on women's tenure compared to men's. The not-statistically-significant negative coefficient for the *Seat Change* variable indicates that men are not punished for seat losses, and the coefficient for the interaction variable suggests that

---

[34] In Figure 14 we run two separate models because we lose many cases when we include the polling variable.

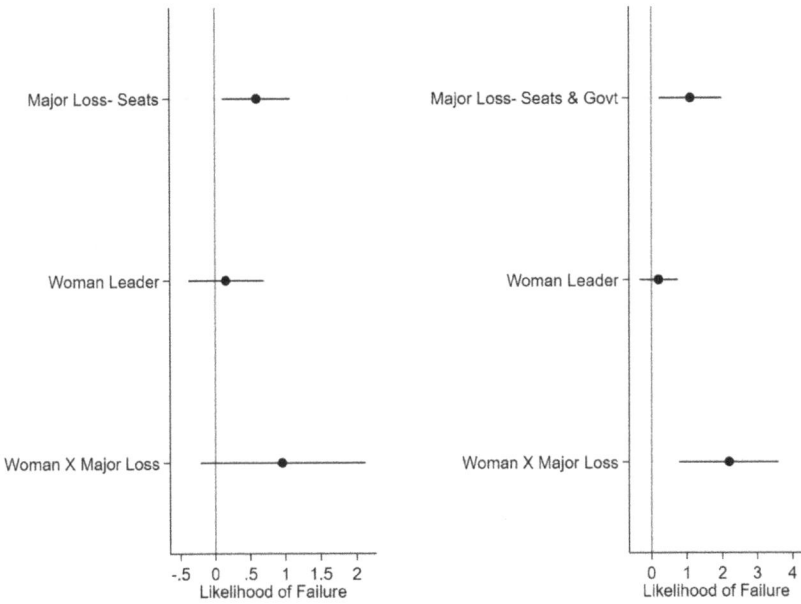

Figure 15 Performance effects on leader tenures – major loss.

Note: The coefficients and the standard errors (with 90% confidence intervals) come from the fully specified interaction models with all the control variables. The left-side graph shows the effect of Major Loss, defined as losing more than 10% seat share, and the right-side graph shows the effect of Major Loss, defined as losing more than 10% seat share and the government status.

women and men are treated significantly differently for seat changes. The negative interaction coefficient tells us that women are punished for seat losses and awarded for seat gains, and these effects are significantly different than the effect of seat change on men's tenure. Government Loss and Poll Change, on the other hand, do not have varying effects on women or men leaders' tenures (the interactions are not statistically significant). The likelihood of men failing increases by 2.8 times when they lose government status, and women similarly are more at risk of failing for government loss.

One may argue that these not-significant interaction coefficients, along with the not-significant coefficients in Figure 12 for the government and polling effects on women's tenure, suggest that only men get punished/awarded for these performance downturns/upticks. We note, however, that the not-statistically-significant interaction coefficients do not mean that women are *not* punished/awarded for government or polling changes; rather, men and women are not treated differently in this regard. They are both punished for government and polling losses. The potential reason why the coefficients for these variables are not significant in Figure 12 is likely because when we test the models separately for women and men, our sample sizes are 2,476 (without polling) and 1,088 (with polling) for the women-only models (as opposed to 10.016 and 7,392 for men), increasing the sizes of standard errors significantly.

Moving to the next set of results, the left-side graph in Figure 15 shows that losing 10% or more seat share similarly harms women and men. The coefficient for the major loss variable is positive and statistically significant, indicating men are punished for a large seat loss, but the interaction effect is not significant, suggesting that there is no difference between how women and men are treated following a major seat loss. However, the right-side graph shows that a major seat loss of 10% or more combined with government loss has more detrimental effects on women. Men also get punished (the major loss variable is positive and significant, and the hazard rate suggests that men are three times more likely to fail for a major loss of seats and government). And the positive and significant interaction tells us that women are punished even more, supporting our hypothesis.

Selectorate and Leader Election Effects

According to our second and third hypotheses, larger and more inclusive membership elections, a higher number of candidates, and a higher margin of victory should help women more than men. Women overcome significant challenges when they are elected via membership vote and when they defeat a large slate of candidates, both of which, as a result, likely generate higher legitimacy evaluations for women. Women can also claim a convincing mandate when they have a high margin of victory.

Figure 16 tests the effects of election details and shows that men who are elected through the vote of membership or delegate votes (which we call inclusive selectorate) have a lower likelihood of failure (the coefficient for the inclusive selectorate variable is negative and statistically significant), as we expected. However, there are no gender differences (the interaction variable is not statistically significant), suggesting that there are no gendered effects of the selectorate type on leader survival. These null findings may suggest that while membership elections may improve the legitimacy evaluations of women leaders, they can only keep their office if they placate the smaller party elites with private goods, as the selectorate theory (Bueno de Mesquita et al. 2002) argues.[35]

The results for the number of candidates and margin of victory also go against our expectations. While men who emerged from an election with a

---

[35] We note, however, that later, we see women's and men's effects significantly differ for inclusive elections when we consider the conditioning effects of performance.

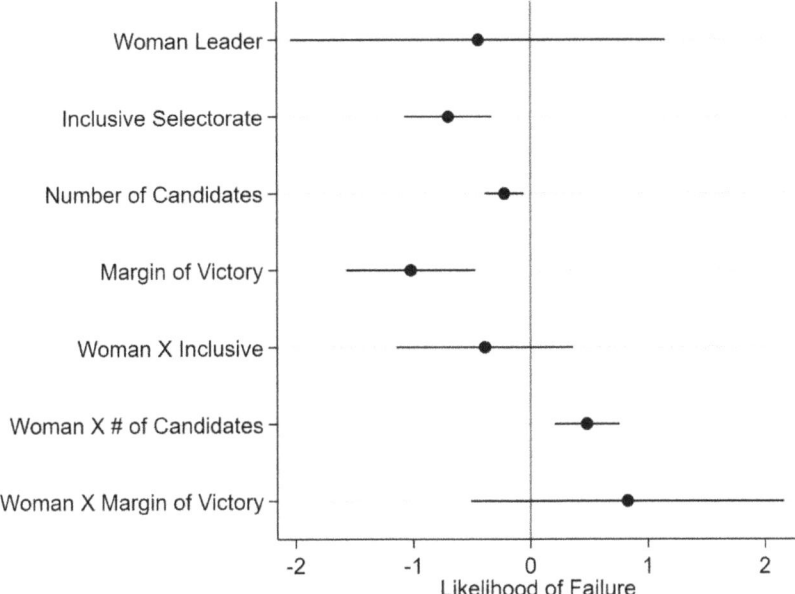

Figure 16 Selectorate effects on leader tenures.

Note: The coefficients and the standard errors (with 90% confidence intervals) come from the fully specified interaction model where the focus is on the inclusive selectorate, number of candidates, and margin of victory variables along with the control variables.

higher number of candidates and who won decisively are less likely to fail in office (both variables' coefficients are negative and statistically significant), women's likelihood to fail in office increases with the number of candidates, and the difference is significant. There is no statistical difference between men and women for the effects of the margin of victory.

The number of candidate effects goes against our hypothesis and suggests that winning in a leadership election with a large slate of candidates likely helps men establish their authority over the party and their legitimacy and helps them keep their position longer. On the other hand, the smaller the pool, the better for the elected woman leader. What explains this latter effect? We speculate that there may be two reasons why small pools are better for women (and note that the majority of our women leaders were elected in single-candidate races): first, they may be taking on a high-risk, weak party which takes time to recover and others are unwilling to rise up until it recovers. Second, a woman, elected in a smaller slate, may suggest a very high-quality/competent candidate who has dominance over the party, and who might be risky and hard to challenge by others.

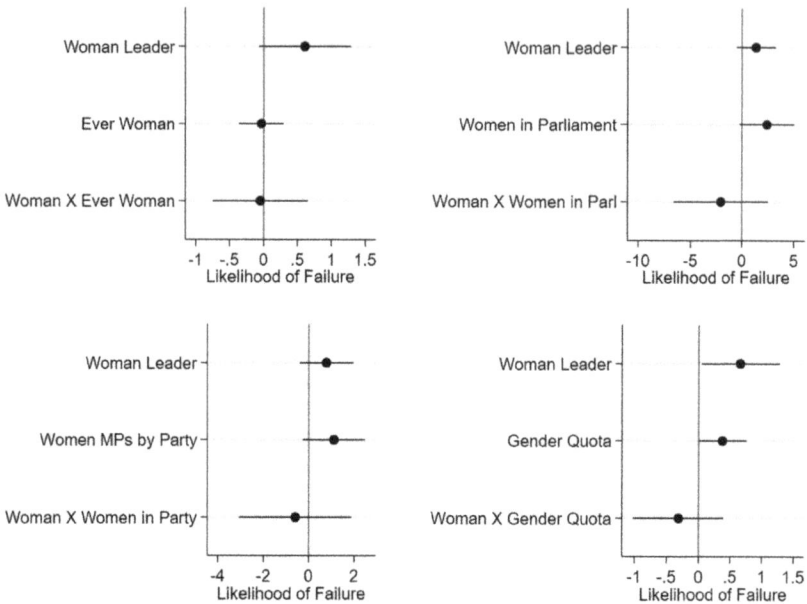

Figure 17 Culture effects on leader tenures.

Note: The coefficients and the standard errors (with 90% confidence intervals) come from the fully specified separate interaction model where the focus is on the four gender-inclusive political culture variables along with the control variables.

Political Culture

According to H4, we expect the gender-inclusive political culture to help women survive longer in office. Figure 17 presents the results for each political culture variable separately (due to the high correlation between some). None of the political culture variables significantly help women more than men for their tenure (none of the interactions are significant). These results are interesting, as we found significant effects of political culture variables on the candidacy and selection of women in Section 3. It appears that while the inclusive culture is important for helping women rise in the party and become leaders, it does not necessarily help women keep their office once they are elected.

Testing the Moderation Hypotheses

We now turn our attention to the analyses of the conditioning effects of the party performance to test H2a (the positive effects of the inclusive membership or delegate vote dissipate (strengthen) when there is a performance downturn (uptick)) and H3a (the positive effects of election details on women's tenure weaken (strengthen) when the leader performs poorly (well)). We use seat change (i.e., the only performance variable that affects the tenures of women and men differently) to test these conditional hypotheses. We then test the conditioning effects of inclusiveness of political culture to examine our last hypothesis, H4a (the gendered tenure differences due to performance, electorate, and competition are particularly pronounced in systems with limited women representation in politics). For these models, we interacted our key variables with the party share of women MPs due to our expectation that party share of women MPs is the most direct measure for gender-inclusive culture in the party.[36]

We run triple interaction models between our key variables, gender dummy variables, and the conditioning variable to test the conditioning effects. Due to high multicollinearity concerns between the consecutive parts, we run each triple interaction in separate models while adding all other variables as control variables. The full triple interactions are reported in the online Appendix.

Out of the three triple interaction models we ran to check the conditioning effects of performance (i.e., seat change) for the effects of inclusive selectorate, the number of candidates, and the margin of victory, only the triple interaction between the seat change, gender dummy, and inclusive selectorate dummy produces significant effects. To recap what we found earlier in the original models, the results showed that inclusive selectorates help both men and women to survive longer in office with no statistically significant difference between men and women. The new conditioning effect model, the key variables of which we report in Figure 18, shows that when membership/delegates decide on party leadership, if the seat change is negative (performance is down), the failure rate of women significantly increases compared to that of men (the triple interaction is negative and statistically significant), for whom inclusive selectorates do not have any effects during performance downturns (the inclusive and seat change interaction is not statistically significant). Similarly, when parties gain seat shares, inclusive selectorates especially help women to keep their office. These results support H2a. However, we do not find any support for H3a given that there are no statistically significant conditioning effects of performance for the election details (see the online Appendix for these results).

For the conditioning effects of political culture, we tested five triple interaction models by interacting the party share of women MPs variable with the gender dummy and separately with (1) seat change, (2) government loss, (3) inclusive selectorate, (4) number of candidates, and (5) margin of victory variables. As can be seen in the online Appendix, none of the triple interactions were statistically significant. Therefore, we do not find support for H4a.

---

[36] We cannot use the ever-woman dummy variable for these analyses due to the limited variation and high multicollinearity it causes in the triple interaction models.

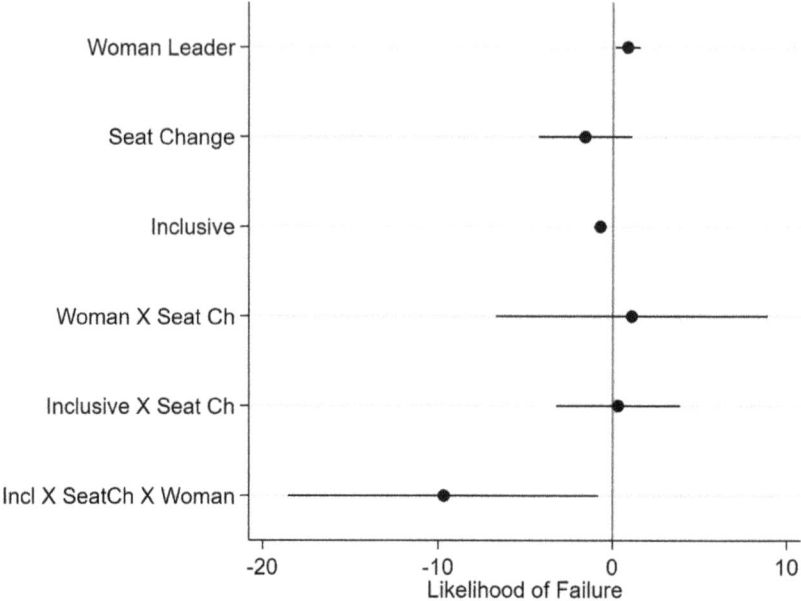

Figure 18 Joint effects of gender, seat change, and selectorate inclusiveness on leader.

Note: The coefficients come from the models where the focus is on the two major loss variables, along with the control variables.

All models we have reported so far included the following control variables, as we described in the research design section: party government status, leader age, a dummy variable for the left parties of social democratic, green, and left-libertarian parties, a decade dummy for the 2000s and 2010s, a dummy for the leader-centric countries of Australia, Canada, Germany, Ireland, and the United Kingdom, and the interaction of this leader-centric systems variable with the gender dummy.[37] Party government status, leader age, and the leader-centric interaction variable with gender consistently produced statistically significant and expected coefficients for all the preceding models. Leader tenures are shorter when parties are not in the government, when the leaders are older, and in the more party-centric systems of Europe. The remaining control variables rarely produce statistically significant effects across all these models and do not have consistent signs for the coefficients.

Conclusion

While the average tenures for women and men leaders in our dataset are similar, we have shown in this section that seat changes, selectorate inclusiveness,

---

[37] The full results can be found the online Appendix.

and the number of candidates for party leader elections have different effects on women leaders' tenures compared to men's. Women are punished for seat losses more than men but also are rewarded more for seat gains, and major losses significantly hurt women more. Leader selection factors showed mixed support for our hypotheses. More inclusive selectorates of members and delegates do not appear to have different effects for men and women party leaders when performance is held constant. However, in the conditional effect models, we saw that the selectorate inclusiveness improves women's tenure more than it does men's if the leader improves the party's performance in office but helps women less to keep their office compared to men if they experience performance downturns following leadership elections, as we expected. The crowdedness of the candidate pool for the leadership election, on the other hand, hurts women's tenure more than men's, which was a finding that goes against our expectation that emerging as the winner from a crowded slate grants women higher legitimacy. Our tentative explanation for this finding is that tenure is likely higher for women if they were elected in races in which they did not face opposition, and when others are less willing to challenge, either because circumstances are risky or because the only woman candidate has high competence/dominance.

Political culture produced null effects throughout this section. The gender-inclusive political culture does not affect women's tenure any differently than men's and does not condition how other variables affect women's tenure. These are interesting null findings, as we clearly saw in Section 3 that political culture significantly affects women's candidacy and selection. However, when it comes to tenure, political culture does not appear to affect women's tenure any differently than men's. Perhaps this is because a woman shatters the glass ceilings by becoming the leader and, regardless of the existing gender-inclusiveness of the political culture in their party and in the parliament, once they become a leader, the cultural restrictions no longer apply to them. Margaret Thatcher was the Tory leader for 15 years when the party share of women MPs was around 3–4% throughout her tenure and the parliamentary share of women MPs was around 3–6%. She shattered an important glass ceiling and, having achieved that, this helped her to keep her position during a time when women were not seen as fit for political office.

These findings take the existing literature forward and contribute to our understanding of gendered patterns of leader tenure. O'Brien's seminal work (2015) showed us that seat changes are more detrimental for women compared to men. We showed robust findings for the seat change effects using an extended dataset up to 2020. But in addition to seat changes, we argued that women's tenure is like quicksand. Several factors, in addition to performance in office, can agitate the sand and make women sink. The selection process and election details also matter (although the gender-inclusiveness of the political culture does not). Examining the tenure of women leaders requires a broader perspective, taking into account several factors related to the selection process and performance in office.

5 Conclusion
The Gendered Life Cycle of Political Leaders

In this Element we examined the life cycle of women political leaders by exploring when they enter the leadership elections as candidates, when they are selected as leaders, and when they lose their posts. This has given us unique insight, using novel data, into one of the most important aspects of political party life. Understanding how women and men reach this post is increasingly more important as politics becomes more personalized and party leaders yield more power. We hypothesized that party performance, the details of the leadership elections and the gender-inclusiveness of the political culture would produce differential impacts on leadership life cycles across women and men. The preponderance of evidence offered here largely supports our hypotheses but also highlights interesting exceptions. Our dataset shows support for the glass ceiling theory that women are less represented in leadership positions than men, but limited and contradicting evidence for the glass cliff theory that women become party leaders following poor party performance. At the same time, our results on women's tenure as party leaders suggest that glass cliffs may still be present for women during their time in office. Our findings also support our original quicksand theory that there are several factors that agitate women's tenure differently than men.

To briefly summarize our findings, following the glass cliff theory (Ryan, Haslam, and Kulich 2010; Ryan and Haslam 2007) and the previous research on women as party leaders, we expected performance downturns to increase the probability that a woman runs for and becomes the party leader. What we found is that when the previous leaders resign due to performance factors, women are more likely to run for party leadership but not necessarily win the leadership post. In terms of leadership tenure, we do find that women are subject to higher stakes and sink into the quicksand of party leadership faster than men following poor party performance, also supporting the glass cliff theory.

Moving to the selection structure and competition, we found that women are more likely to become candidates yet less likely to be elected as leaders when the leadership elections are inclusive, that is, when the membership and/or local delegates, as opposed to the party elites, vote on leaders. In some ways, this might be a discouraging result, showing us that women are set up for failure from the candidacy stage. However, given women often face less competition than men, we could actually view inclusive elections as a pathway to power. For many parties in our data, once women are leading candidates, leadership elections are merely rubber stamps for them, and those who are elected unopposed or with very limited competition enjoy a long tenure in office. Thus, the positive impact of inclusive selection for encouraging women's inclusion is actually a substantial and important conclusion for the party leader literature.

Beyond the performance and electoral/structural factors, we also examined the direct and conditioning effects of political culture and particularly the descriptive representation of women in politics and the party for the life cycle of women in party leadership. Our analyses revealed that women-inclusive parliaments (i.e. those with greater women's representation both in the parliament and within a party's parliamentary delegation) are associated with a higher likelihood that women run for and win leadership positions, although there are no effects of inclusive political culture on women's tenure once elected. Our results suggest that gender-inclusive factors help women shatter the glass ceiling but neither help nor hurt them as they struggle on the quicksand of party leadership tenure.

Implications and Contributions

An exciting and growing literature focuses on how political careers are gendered (Aldrich and Daniel 2024, 2020; Escobar-Lemmon and Taylor-Robinson 2009; Krook and O'Brien 2012) and how party leadership follows similar gendered processes (Dingler and Helms 2023; Morgenroth et al. 2020; O'Brien 2015; O'Neill and Stewart 2009; O'Neill, Pruysers, and Stewart 2021; Thomas 2018). Our Element contributes to this growing literature and pushes this research forward in several ways.

First, we focus on the complete cycle of gendered party leadership, from candidacy to selection and removal, and show varying and often contradicting explanations for how performance, political culture, and selection structures affect these stages differently. Our results suggest that examining women's leadership without understanding the factors behind candidacy, election, and removal in connection with each other only provides a partial picture of women's leadership careers.

Second, we put to the test the existing glass ceiling theory that explains why we see few women in leadership positions and the glass cliff theory on how parties' crises and performance downturns open the way for women to high-risk leadership positions with our original data across 11 democracies and 40 years. While the descriptive and empirical evidence shows that there are still structural (e.g., selectorate type) and cultural factors that limit women's access to candidacy and leadership (and indeed women are still underrepresented in party leadership positions and the races for these positions), which supports the glass ceiling theory, we found that glass cliffs exist for women mostly in the candidacy and tenure stages, not generalizing to the election of women as leaders.

Third, we introduced a new theory of quicksand, explaining how women's survival in office is like standing on quicksand, where various structural, cultural, and performance factors agitate their standing and make them sink faster than men. We found that performance factors are still more detrimental for women. Nevertheless, selectorate type and competition can also have detrimental effects on women, especially when combined with performance downturns, supporting our theory. We also found that the inclusiveness of political culture has no impact on tenure, suggesting that once women break the glass ceiling, their tenure lengths are not influenced by how descriptively represented women are in politics.

Another contribution we made throughout the Element was expanding the focus on performance effects beyond just seat losses. Our original data allowed us to use the resignation reasons of party leaders as reported in the media and discussed by the resigning leaders. This more qualitative performance indicator had significant effects on women's candidacy in Section 3. In addition, building on the recent literature showing the importance of office performance (Ennser-Jedenastik and Schumacher 2021) (beyond just electoral performance), we examined the consequences of changes in government status and polling standing on women's candidacy, election, and survival. While these are influential for all leaders, regardless of their gender, our results highlighted the significantly different effects of seat changes for women and men. Government status changes and polling, on the other hand, have similar effects on women's and men's tenures.

Fifth, our results contribute to a growing literature on the consequences of leadership election details on leader evaluations and tenure (Astudillo and Paneque 2022; Matthews and Whiting 2022; Verge and Astudillo 2019). We used extended data coverage and analyzed the gendered effects of party organizational features, such as the type of selectorate and the extent of leadership election competition, on the complete life cycle of women leaders, which is a unique contribution of our study.

Finally, as one of our most important contributions, we showed that women's careers as political party leaders have three interrelated but also very distinct stages that have their own gendered patterns. Without women running for office, they cannot get elected. Yet, factors that improve their numbers among the leadership candidates, such as inclusive membership elections, may hurt them in leadership elections. Performance downturns do not define women's election to leadership, but have substantive impacts on their candidacy and tenure. Women's descriptive political representation is critical for their candidacy and selection but does not improve their tenure. Putting together these different stages of women's careers as leaders, therefore, helps us better understand the mitigating and encouraging factors to improve women's representation in these most significant positions within political parties.

What's Next?

In this Element, we offered an analysis of leadership samples that considered all leadership changes in our data and those that included at least one woman, but we still did not find a consistent and expected relationship between our other performance measures and women's leadership, i.e. for the glass cliff theory. One possibility is that the reason for the lack of consistent evidence is because we still have relatively few women in our data compared to men. While we are able to highlight the modal conditions for women's leadership success, their numbers are still dwarfed by men, supporting the glass ceiling theory. Until we have more women in our data, and especially leadership contests that include both women and men, it may continue to be difficult to derive the general conditions that make women's success likely. As women's leadership becomes more common (and the numbers have been growing in recent decades), the opportunities to study these patterns in more detail will grow.

Additional data on women leaders will also open up new opportunities to examine additional interesting questions that we did not have the space or opportunity to study. How do different demographic features (e.g., age, masculinity) and background characteristics (e.g., seniority/ political experience) of women affect their likelihood of running for, getting elected to, and keeping the party leadership positions? Dingler and Helms (2023) show with a focus on opposition party leaders across 28 countries that previous political experience does not matter. We could not test this in our sample of 58 women leaders. However, one way forward is to examine how the descriptive and career-based characteristics affect women leaders.

Inclusive, registered-members-based elections are also becoming increasingly more common across the parliamentary systems. While the evidence from the United States primary literature suggests that the negative effects of primaries, with their blood-on-the-floor effects, may only apply to races featuring an incumbent rather than contests for an open seat, like the party leadership elections (Johnson, Petersheim, and Wasson 2010), we found that membership elections still hurt women when it comes to their election to the position. An interesting direction for future research is whether this effect persists as membership elections become more common in countries where delegates have been electing more women leaders, such as in Scandinavia, and especially as the perceptions of women in leadership positions are changing. While recent work by Chen et al. (2023) shows that men are still seen as naturally better fits for leadership positions in Canada, Van Der Pas, Aaldering, and Bos (2023) show with a list experiment in the United States that women politicians are associated with more positive traits. Therefore, further analyses of changing gender stereotypes and their conditioning effects on the increasingly more open leadership elections are needed.

Finally, our focus in this Element was on understanding whether there are gendered patterns that explain women's candidacy, leadership, and tenure as party leaders when compared to men. However, the other side of the picture is when men decide to stay out of the leadership race and when they challenge an incumbent woman. While we decided not to analyze these interesting questions, the descriptive evidence suggests that men stay out of those races women win, and are unlikely to challenge women leaders if women win their positions unopposed. Future research can benefit from examination of these interesting questions on men's strategic behaviors, given their potential consequences for women party leaders.

References

Aldrich, Andrea S. 2020. "Party Organization and Gender in European Elections." *Party Politics* 26(5):675–688.

Aldrich, Andrea S., Joseph Francesco Cozza, Gonzalo Di Landro, and Zeynep Somer-Topcu. 2023. "Participation, Gender, and Legitimacy in Party Leader Selection." Lecture presented on February 6, 2024, at the European Institute, The London School of Economics and Political Science.

Aldrich, Andrea S., and Lauren K. Perez. 2021. "Losing Women, Losing Power? Gender, Turnover, and EU Legislation." In *Personnel Turnover and the Legitimacy of the EU*, ed. John A. Scherpereel. Cham: Springer International Publishing pp. 107–135.

Aldrich, Andrea S., and William T. Daniel. 2020. "The Consequences of Quotas: Assessing the Effect of Varied Gender Quotas on Legislator Experience in the European Parliament." *Politics & Gender* 16(3):738–767.

Aldrich, Andrea S., and William T. Daniel. 2024. "Gender Quota Adoption and the Qualifications of Parliamentarians." *The Journal of Politics* 86(2):798–803.

Aldrich, Andrea S., and William T. Daniel. 2025. *Quotas as Game Changers for the Recruitment, Selection, and Performance of Elected Politicians*. Oxford: Oxford University Press.

Alexander, Rohan. 2021. "A Dataset of Australian Federal Politicians (1901–2021) and Associated R Package." https://CRAN.R-project.org/package=AustralianPoliticians. Last updated November 29, 2021.

Alt, James E., and Gary King. 1994. "Transfers of Governmental Power: The Meaning of Time Dependence." *Comparative Political Studies* 27(2):190–210.

Andrews, Josephine T., and Robert W. Jackman. 2008. "If Winning Isn't Everything, Why Do They Keep Score? Consequences of Electoral Performance for Party Leaders." *British Journal of Political Science* 38(4):657–675.

Armstrong, Brenna, Tiffany D. Barnes, Daina Chiba, and Diana Z. O'Brien. 2023. "Financial Crises and the Selection and Survival of Women Finance Ministers." *American Political Science Review* 118(3):1305–1323.

Astudillo, Javier, and Andreu Paneque. 2022. "Do Party Primaries Punish Women? Revisiting the Trade-off between the Inclusion of Party Members and the Selection of Women as Party Leaders." *Party Politics* 28(3):496–506.

References

Astudillo, Javier, and Ignacio Lago. 2021. "Primaries through the Looking Glass: The Electoral Effects of Opening the Selection of Top Candidates." *British Journal of Political Science* 51(4):1550–1564.

Banducci, Susan A., and Jeffrey A. Karp. 2000. "Gender, Leadership and Choice in Multiparty Systems." *Political Research Quarterly* 53(4):815–848.

Barnes, Tiffany D., and Diana Z. O'Brien. 2018. "Defending the Realm: The Appointment of Female Defense Ministers Worldwide." *American Journal of Political Science* 62(2):355–368.

Bashevkin, Sylvia. 2009. "Party Talk: Assessing the Feminist Rhetoric of Women Leadership Candidates in Canada." *Canadian Journal of Political Science/Revue canadienne de science politique* 42(2):345–362.

Baumann, Markus, Hanna Bäck, and Johan Bo Davidsson. 2019. "Double Standards: The Role of Gender and Intraparty Politics in Swedish Cabinet Appointments." *Politics & Gender* 15(4):882–911.

Beckwith, Karen. 2015. "Before Prime Minister: Margaret Thatcher, Angela Merkel, and Gendered Party Leadership Contests." *Politics & Gender* 11(04):718–745.

Berlinski, Samuel, Torun Dewan, and Keith Dowding. 2007. "The Length of Ministerial Tenure in the United Kingdom, 1945–97." *British Journal of Political Science* 37(2):245–262.

Bille, Lars. 1997. "Leadership Change and Party Change: The Case of the Danish Social Democratic Party, 1960–95." *Party Politics* 3(3):379–390.

Bittner, Amanda. 2011. *Platform or Personality? The Role of Party Leaders in Elections*. Oxford: Oxford University Press.

Bjarnegård, Elin. 2013. *Gender, Informal Institutions and Political Recruitment*. London: Palgrave Macmillan UK.

Blumenau, Jack. 2021. "The Effects of Female Leadership on Women's Voice in Political Debate." *British Journal of Political Science* 51(2):750–771.

Bridgewater, Jack, and Robert Ulrich Nagel. 2020. "Is There Cross-national Evidence That Voters Prefer Men as Party Leaders? No." *Electoral Studies* 67:102209.

Bueno de Mesquita, Bruce, Alastair Smith, Randolph M. Siverson, and James D. Morrow. 2002. *The Logic of Political Survival*. New York: MIT Press.

Caul, Miki. 1999. "Women's Representation in Parliament: The Role of Political Parties." *Party Politics* 5(1):79–98.

Chen, Philip, Melanee Thomas, Allison Harell, and Tania Gosselin. 2023. "Explicit Gender Stereotyping in Canadian Politics." *Canadian Journal of Political Science* 56(1):209–221.

Conover, Pamela Johnston, and Virginia Gray. 1983. *Feminism and the New Right: Conflict over the American Family*. Westport, CT: Praeger.

Cozza, Joseph Francesco, Gonzalo Di Landro, and Zeynep Somer-Topcu. 2023. "Competitive Party Leadership Elections and Their Consequences for Leader Evaluations."

Cozza, Joseph Francesco, and Zeynep Somer-Topcu. 2021. "Membership Vote for Party Leadership Changes: Electoral Effects and the Causal Mechanisms Behind." *Electoral Studies* 71:102326.

Cross, William P., and Andre Blais. 2012. *Politics at the Center: The Selection and Removal of Party Leaders in the Anglo Parliamentary Democracies*. Oxford: Oxford University Press.

Cross, William P., Katz Richard S., and Pruysers, Scott. 2018. *The Personalization of Democratic Politics and the Challenge for Political Parties*. Colchester, UK: ECPR Press.

Dassonneville, Ruth, Stephen Quinlan, and Ian McAllister. 2021. "Female Leader Popularity and the Vote, 1996–2016: A Global Exploratory Analysis." *European Journal of Politics and Gender* 4(3):341–359.

Davidson-Schmich, Louise K., 2015. *A Glass Half Full: Gender Quotas and Political Recruitment in Germany*. Ann Arbor, MI: University of Michigan Press.

Davidson-Schmich, Louise K., Farida Jalalzai, and Malliga Och. 2023. "Crisis, Gender Role Congruency, and Perceptions of Executive Leadership." *Politics & Gender* 19(3):1–8.

Davis, Rebecca Howard. 1997. *Women and Power in Parliamentary Democracies: Cabinet Appointments in Western Europe, 1968–1992*. Lincoln, NE: University of Nebraska Press.

Devroe, Robin, and Sigrid Van Trappen. 2022. "Keeping Women in Their Place? The Prevalence of Gender Role Attitudes among Local Party Chairs in Flanders." *Acta Politica* 57(3):472–488.

Dingler, Sarah C., and Ludger Helms. 2023. "Parliamentary Women Opposition Leaders: A Comparative Assessment across 28 OECD Countries." *Politics and Governance* 11(1):85–96.

Ennser-Jedenastik, Laurenz, and Gijs Schumacher. 2015. Why Some Leaders Die Hard (and Others Don't). In *The Politics of Party Leadership*, ed. William Cross and Jean-Benoit Pilet. Oxford: Oxford University Press pp. 107–127.

Ennser-Jedenastik, Laurenz, and Woflgang C. Müller. 2015. "Intra-Party Democracy, Political Performance and the Survival of Party Leaders: Austria, 1945–2011." *Party Politics*, 21(6):930–943.

Ennser-Jedenastik, Laurenz, and Gijs Schumacher. 2021. "What Parties Want from their Leaders: How Office Achievement Trumps Electoral Performance as a Driver of Party Leader Survival." *European Journal of Political Research* 60(1):114–130.

Escobar-Lemmon, Maria C., and Michelle M. Taylor-Robinson. 2016. *Women in Presidential Cabinets: Power Players or Abundant Tokens?* Oxford: Oxford University Press.

Escobar-Lemmon, Maria C., and Michelle M. Taylor-Robinson. 2009. "Getting to the Top: Career Paths of Women in Latin American Cabinets." *Political Research Quarterly* 62(4):685–699.

Folke, Olle, and Johanna Rickne. 2016. "The Glass Ceiling in Politics: Formalization and Empirical Tests." *Comparative Political Studies* 49(5):567–599.

Fox, Richard L., and Jennifer L. Lawless. 2011. "Gendered Perceptions and Political Candidacies: A Central Barrier to Women's Equality in Electoral Politics." *American Journal of Political Science* 55(1):59–73.

Fox, Richard L., and Zoe M. Oxley. 2003. "Gender Stereotyping in State Executive Elections: Candidate Selection and Success." *Journal of Politics* 65(3):833–850.

Franceschet, Susan, Mona Lena Krook, and Jennifer M. Piscopo. 2012. *The Impact of Gender Quotas*. Oxford: Oxford University Press.

Funk, Kendall D., Magda Hinojosa, and Jennifer M. Piscopo. 2019. "Women to the Rescue: The Gendered Effects of Public Discontent on Legislative Nominations in Latin America." *Party Politics* 27(3). DOI: https://doi.org/10.1177/1354068819856614.

Garzia, Diego. 2011. "The Personalization of Politics in Western Democracies: Causes and Consequences on Leader–Follower Relationships." *The Leadership Quarterly* 22(4):697–709.

Garzia, Diego, Frederico Ferreira Da Silva, and Andrea De Angelis. 2022. "Partisan Dealignment and the Personalisation of Politics in West European Parliamentary Democracies, 1961–2018." *West European Politics* 45(2):311–334.

Holman, Mirya R., Jennifer L. Merolla, and Elizabeth J. Zechmeister. 2011. "Sex, Stereotypes, and Security: A Study of the Effects of Terrorist Threat on Assessments of Female Leadership." *Journal of Women, Politics & Policy* 32(3):173–192.

Huidobro, Alba, and Albert Falcó-Gimeno. 2023. "Women Who Win But Do Not Rule: The Effect of Gender in the Formation of Governments." *The Journal of Politics* 85(4):1562–1568.

Jalalzai, Farida, and Mona Lena Krook. 2010. "Beyond Hillary and Benazir: Women's Political Leadership Worldwide." *International Political Science Review* 31(1):5–21.

Jennings, William, and Christopher Wlezien. 2016. "The Timeline of Elections: A Comparative Perspective." *American Journal of Political Science* 60(1):2019–2233.

Johnson, Gregg B., Meredith-Joy Petersheim, and Jesse T. Wasson. 2010. "Divisive Primaries and Incumbent General Election Performance: Prospects and Costs in U.S. House Races." *American Politics Research* 38(5):931–955.

Kanthak, Kristin, and Jonathan Woon. 2015. "Women Don't Run? Election Aversion and Candidate Entry." *American Journal of Political Science* 59(3):595–612.

Kenig, Ofer. 2009. "Democratization of Party Leadership Selection: Do Wider Selectorates Produce More Competitive Contests?" *Electoral Studies* 28(2):240–247.

Kenny, Meryl, and Tània Verge. 2013. "Decentralization, Political Parties, and Women's Representation: Evidence from Spain and Britain." *Publius: The Journal of Federalism* 43(1):109–128.

Kittilson, Miki Caul. 2011. "Women, Parties and Platforms in Post-industrial Democracies." *Party Politics* 17(1):66–92.

Kroeber, Corinna. 2022. "How Parties Led by a Woman Redefine Their Positions: Empirical Evidence for Women's Green, Alternative and Libertarian Agenda." *European Journal of Political Research* 61(1):175–193.

Krook, Mona Lena. 2010. *Quotas for Women in Politics: Gender and Candidate Selection Reform Worldwide*. Oxford: Oxford University Press.

Krook, Mona Lena, and Diana Z. O'Brien. 2012. "All the President's Men? The Appointment of Female Cabinet Ministers Worldwide." *The Journal of Politics* 74(3):840–855.

Lago, Ignacio, and Javier Astudillo. 2023. "Selecting Party Leaders." *West European Politics* 48(1):165–188.

Lawless, Jennifer L. 2004. "Women, War, and Winning Elections: Gender Stereotyping in the Post-September 11th Era." *Political Research Quarterly* 57(3):479–490.

LeDuc, Lawrence. 2001. "Democratizing Party Leadership Selection." *Party Politics* 7(3):323–341.

Magalhães, Pedro C., and Miguel M. Pereira. 2024. "Women Running for Office Are Less Risk Averse than Men: Evidence from Portugal." *The Journal of Politics* 86(3):1093–1097.

Matthews, Neil, and Sophie Whiting. 2022. "'To the Surprise of Absolutely No One': Gendered Political Leadership Change in Northern Ireland." *The British Journal of Politics and International Relations* 24(2):224–242.

Morgenroth, Thekla, Teri A. Kirby, Michelle K. Ryan, and Antonia Sudkämper. 2020. "The Who, When, and Why of the Glass Cliff Phenomenon: A Meta-analysis of Appointments to Precarious Leadership Positions." *Psychological Bulletin* 146(9):797–829.

Mughan, Anthony. 2000. *Media and the Presidentialization of Parliamentary Elections*. London: Palgrave.

Niven, David. 1998. "Party Elites and Women Candidates: The Shape of Bias." *Women & Politics* 19(2):57–80.

Norris, Pippa, ed. 2010. *Cracking the Highest Glass Ceiling: A Global Comparison of Women's Campaigns for Executive Office*. Santa Barbara, CA: Bloomsbury Publishing.

O'Brien, Diana Z. 2015. "Rising to the Top: Gender, Political Performance, and Party Leadership in Parliamentary Democracies." *American Journal of Political Science* 59(4):1022–1039.

O'Brien, Diana Z. 2019. "Female Leaders and Citizens' Perceptions of Political Parties." *Journal of Elections, Public Opinion and Parties* 29(4):465–489.

O'Brien, Diana Z., and Jennifer M. Piscopo. 2019. The Impact of Women in Parliament. In *The Palgrave Handbook of Women's Political Rights*. London: Palgrave MacMillan, pp. 53–72.

O'Brien, Diana Z., Matthew Mendez, Jordan Carr Peterson, and Jihyun Shin. 2015. "Letting Down the Ladder or Shutting the Door: Female Prime Ministers, Party Leaders, and Cabinet Ministers." *Politics & Gender* 11(04):689–717.

O'Neill, Brenda, and David K. Stewart. 2009. "Gender and Political Party Leadership in Canada." *Party Politics* 15(6):737–757.

O'Neill, Brenda, Scott Pruysers, and David K Stewart. 2021. "Glass Cliffs or Partisan Pressure? Examining Gender and Party Leader Tenures and Exits." *Political Studies* 69(2):257–277.

Paxton, Pamela, Jennifer Green, and Melanie Hughes. 2008. *Women in Parliament, 1945–2003: Cross-national Dataset*. Ann Arbor, MI: Inter-university Consortium for Political and Social Research.

Pedersen, Karina, and Tim Knudsen. 2005. Denmark: Presidentialization in a Consensual Democracy. In *The Presidentialization of Politics: A Comparative Study of Modern Democracies*, ed. Thomas Poguntke and Paul Webb. Oxford: Oxford University Press, pp. 159–175.

Perdue, Abigail. 2016. "Man up or Go Home: Exploring Perceptions of Women in Leadership." *Marquette Law Review* 100(4):1233–1308.

Poguntke, Thomas, and Paul Webb, eds. 2005. *The Presidentialization of Politics: A Comparative Study of Modern Democracies*. Oxford: Oxford Univeristy Press.

Rahat, Gideon, and Reuven Y. Hazan. 2010. *Democracy within Parties: Candidate Selection Methods and Thier Political Consquences*. Oxford: Oxford University Press.

Ryan, Michelle K., and S. Alexander Haslam. 2005. "The Glass Cliff: Evidence That Women are Over-represented in Precarious Leadership Positions." *British Journal of Management* 16(2):81–90.

Ryan, Michelle K., and S. Alexander Haslam. 2007. "The Glass Cliff: Exploring the Dynamics Surrounding the Appointment of Women to Precarious Leadership Positions." *Academy of Mangement Review* 32(2):549–572.

Ryan, Michelle K., S. Alexander Haslam, and Clara Kulich. 2010. "Politics and the Glass Cliff: Evidence That Women Are Preferentially Selected to Contest Hard-to-Win Seats." *Psychology of Women Quarterly* 34(1):56–64.

Ryan, Michelle K., S. Alexander Haslam, Thekla Morgenroth, Floor Rink, Janka Stoker, and Kim Peters. 2016. "Getting on Top of the Glass Cliff: Reviewing a Decade of Evidence, Explanations, and Impact." *The Leadership Quarterly* 27(3):446–455.

Sanbonmatsu, Kira. 2002. "Gender Stereotypes and Vote Choice." *American Journal of Political Science* 46(1):20–34.

Schneider, Monica C., Mirya R. Holman, Amanda B. Diekman, and Thomas McAndrew. 2016. "Power, Conflict, and Community: How Gendered Views of Political Power Influence Women's Political Ambition." *Political Psychology* 37(4):515–531.

Schwindt-Bayer, Leslie A. 2009. "Making Quotas Work: The Effect of Gender Quota Laws on the Election of Women." *Legislative Studies Quarterly* 34(1):5–28.

Somer-Topcu, Zeynep. 2017. "Agree or Disagree: How Do Party Leader Changes Affect the Distribution of Voters' Perceptions." *Party Politics* 23(1):66–75.

Somer-Topcu, Zeynep, and Daniel Weitzel. 2023. Leadership Turnovers and Their Electoral Consequences: A Social Democratic Exceptionalism. In *Beyond Social Democracy. The Transformation of the Left in Emerging Knowledge Societies*, ed. Silja Häusermann and Herbert Kitschelt. Cambridge University Press, pp. 366–392.

Stambough, Stephen J., and Valerie R. O'Regan. 2007. "Republican Lambs and the Democratic Pipeline: Partisan Differences in the Nomination of Female Gubernatorial Candidates." *Politics and Gender* 3(03):349–368.

Strøm, Kaare. 1993. "Competition Ruins the Good Life." *European Journal of Political Research* 24(3):317–347.

Thomas, Melanee. 2018. "In Crisis or Decline? Selecting Women to Lead Provincial Parties in Government." *Canadian Journal of Political Science* 51(2):379–403.

Van Der Pas, Daphne, Loes Aaldering, and Angela L. Bos. 2023. "Looks Like a Leader: Measuring Evolution in Gendered Politician Stereotypes." *Political Behavior* 46(3):1653–1675.

Verge, Tània, and Javier Astudillo. 2018. "The Gender Politics of Executive Candidate Selection and Reselection." *European Journal of Political Research*, DOI: https://doi.org/10.1111/1475-6765.12312

Verge, Tània, and Javier Astudillo. 2019. "The Gender Politics of Executive Candidate Selection and Reselection." *European Journal of Political Research* 58(2):720–740.

Walther, Daniel, and Johan Hellström. 2019. "The Verdict in the Polls: How Government Stability Is Affected by Popular Support." *West European Politics* 42(3):593–617.

Warwick, Paul V. 1992. "Rising Hazards: An Underlying Dynamic of Parliamentary Government." *American Journal of Political Science* pp. 857–876.

Weeks, Ana Catalano, Bonnie M. Meguid, Miki Caul Kittilson, and Hilde Coffé. 2023. "When Do Männerparteien Elect Women? Radical Right Populist Parties and Strategic Descriptive Representation." *American Political Science Review* 117(2):421–438.

Wolbrecht, Christina, and David E. Campbell. 2007. "Leading by Example: Female Members of Parliament as Political Role Models." *American Journal of Political Science* 51(4):921–939.

Yates, Candida. 2019. "'Show Us You Care!' The Gendered Psycho-Politics of Emotion and Women as Political Leaders." *European Journal of Politics and Gender* 2(3):345–361.

Cambridge Elements =

Gender and Politics

Tiffany D. Barnes
University of Texas at Austin

Tiffany D. Barnes is Professor of Political Science at the University of Texas at Austin. She is the author of *Women, Politics, and Power: A Global Perspective* (Rowman & Littlefield, 2007) and, award-winning, *Gendering Legislative Behavior* (Cambridge University Press, 2016). Her research has been funded by the National Science Foundation (NSF) and recognized with numerous awards. Barnes is the former president of the Midwest Women's Caucus and founder and director of the Empirical Study of Gender (EGEN) network.

Diana Z. O'Brien
Washington University in St. Louis

Diana Z. O'Brien is the Bela Kornitzer Distinguished Professor of Political Science at Washington University in St. Louis. She specializes in the causes and consequences of women's political representation. Her award-winning research has been supported by the NSF and published in leading political science journals. O'Brien has also served as a Fulbright Visiting Professor, an associate editor at *Politics & Gender*, the president of the Midwest Women's Caucus, and a founding member of the EGEN network.

About the Series

From campaigns and elections to policymaking and political conflict, gender pervades every facet of politics. Elements in Gender and Politics features carefully theorized, empirically rigorous scholarship on gender and politics. The Elements both offer new perspectives on foundational questions in the field and identify and address emerging research areas.

Cambridge Elements

Gender and Politics

Elements in the Series

In Love and at War: Marriage in Non-state Armed Groups
Hilary Matfess

Counter-Stereotypes and Attitudes Toward Gender and LGBTQ Equality
Jae-Hee Jung and Margit Tavits

The Politics of Bathroom Access and Exclusion in the United States
Sara Chatfield

Women, Gender, and Rebel Governance during Civil Wars
Meredith Maloof Loken

Abortion Attitudes and Polarization in the American Electorate
Erin C. Cassese, Heather L. Ondercin and Jordan Randall

Gender, Ethnicity, and Intersectionality in Cabinets: Asia and Europe in Comparative Perspective
Amy H. Liu, Roman Hlatky, Keith Padraic Chew, Eoin L. Power, Sam Selsky, Betty Compton and Meiying Xu

Gendered Jobs and Local Leaders: Women, Work, and the Pipeline to Local Political Office
Rachel Bernhard and Mirya R. Holman

What's Happened to the Gender Gap in Political Activity: Social Structure, Politics, and Participation in the United States
Shauna L. Shames, Sara Morell, Ashley Jardina, Kay Lehman Schlozman and Nancy Burns

Family Matters: How Romantic Partners Shape Politicians' Careers
Olle Folke, Moa Frödin Gruneau and Johanna Rickne

Glass Ceilings, Glass Cliffs, and Quicksands: Gendered Party Leadership in Parliamentary Systems
Andrea S. Aldrich and Zeynep Somer-Topcu

A full series listing is available at: www.cambridge.org/EGAP

For EU product safety concerns, contact us at Calle de José Abascal, 56–1°, 28003 Madrid, Spain or eugpsr@cambridge.org.

www.ingramcontent.com/pod-product-compliance
Ingram Content Group UK Ltd.
Pitfield, Milton Keynes, MK11 3LW, UK
UKHW040249200625
459886UK00007B/169